80

ADVENTURES
WITH
GOD

Real Stories of God's Intervention
into Ordinary Lives

Ed Colton

80 ADVENTURES WITH GOD

Real Stories of
God's Intervention into Ordinary Lives

ED C. COLTON

"Oh, that men would give thanks to the Lord for His goodness and for his wonderful works to the children of men" (Psalm 107:20).

"80 Adventures with God are true stories that will impart faith and build faith in a living God who wants to be part of every facet of our lives. We highly recommend reading this book but also thinking deeply on the nature of God, who is love."

DR. and MRS. BROOKS BROWN M.D.
Founders, Brooks Rehabilitation Centers Network

"This is a great book to read to hear story after story of the mighty hand of our loving Father, the great "I AM." He is bigger than any challenge, need, obstacle, or attempt by darkness to separate us from His provision. This book will certainly spark and fan the flame of faith within to see God do the same and greater things in your life with your need. What the Lord has done in many others He will do for you, because He is no respecter of persons."

STEPHEN WOMACK
Director,
First Coast Dream Center

"These true short stories written by Ed Colton are both refreshing and faith building. They are a beautiful reminder that a simple, trusting walk with God brings miraculous results."

BEN GOLDSMITH
Director,
Cru Ministries Jacksonville, Florida

"These stories have inspired me and energized my faith. I have this book on my laptop so I can read the stories over and over to remind me of God's great love for me and my family. Because the Lord Jesus is the same yesterday, today, and forever, I see Jesus operating in these stories with ordinary people accomplishing extraordinary results. This little book of stories is a treasure for anyone who reads it."

JIM YOUNG
Community Outreach Ministry Director
North East District, Florida Conference
United Methodist Church

"There are so many challenges that we face daily and often feel so alone without hope of a positive outcome. Reading 80 Adventures with God one will discover a treasure trove of real-life stories of ordinary experiencing extraordinary miracles through a loving and merciful God. No matter what you are going through, a testimony that relates to your situation can be found bringing hope of a miraculous outcome."

COLIN BLOM
President,
Fuzion International Ministries & Fuzion Bible Institute

"True Stories of the Supernatural 1" is a book of miracles, big and small miracles. And sometimes the smallest miracles are the biggest. For example, to be healed from terminal illness is a miracle that is beyond all human explanation or measurement. But also, all heaven rejoices when one sinner accepts Jesus Christ as Lord and Savior, and to me this too is a miracle beyond human explanation or measurement, a miracle in everyday life that is life changing forever -- not by might or power but by the Holy Spirit of the Lord. So as I read these 80 stories in Ed Colton's book, and my story is one of them, I praise God for the daily miracles He works in the lives of those who trust Him because He loves us with unchanging and never ending love, which for me is the greatest of all miracles."

FRANK PEARCE
frank@pearcejobs.com

ARPress
45 Dan Road Suite 15
Canton MA 02021

Hotline:	1(888) 821-0229
Fax:	1(508) 545-7580

Ordering Information:
Quantity sales. Special discounts are available on quantity purchases by corporations, associations, and others. For details, contact the publisher at the address above.

Printed in the United States of America.

ISBN-13:	Paperback	979-8-89389-079-2
	eBook	979-8-89389-080-8

Library of Congress Control Number: 2024924569

Dedication

This book is dedicated to the Lord Jesus Christ, without whom these stories would not have been possible.

Acknowledgements

To the men and women who have shared their stories of faith and relationship with God with us over the years.

To my wife and partner, Sherry, who has experienced these supernatural encounters of God with me and partnered with me in these many years of ministry.

To my loving daughters Katy Jean and Priscilla Joy, who love our Lord Jesus and have brought us happiness in their dedication to Him.

Introduction

80 Adventures with God is a book about the living God working in the everyday affairs of ordinary people like you and me. There are eighty stories of people overcoming situations that only God could handle with His almighty power. These pages witness to a person's relationship with God and are filled with the response of a loving and faithful God through Jesus Christ. It is my heartfelt desire as you read these stories you come to know and believe in a much greater way all that the Lord Jesus has done for us.

--Ed C. Colton

Contents

80 Adventures with God:

Real Stories of God's Intervention into Ordinary Lives

by Ed Colton

Eighty is said to be Moses' wise and substantial age when he received the Ten Commandments. To go around the world in eighty days, as in the famous story, signifies speed. This book's eighty stories combine sagacity and speed to testify to God's goodness. Although each is a personal account, intriguingly the stories' narrators are, for the most part, not named. God is the subject and agent and, as such, is timelessly trustworthy.The stories read quickly until the last two longer ones, as each is only about a page long. They can be read as daily meditations. Each story ends with a biblical quotation, a confirmation that the stories fulfill God's words.

Many of the stories feature one missionary pastor and his family. Taking place in the Far East, Florida, the American South, and other places and times, they entertain with international flair. People all over the world accept Jesus' salvation, each in a unique way. Some narrators' faith heals them physically or emotionally. In some stories, narrators receive a monetary or material answer to prayer. Miracles of being spared from tragedy or meeting the same person in unexpected places also illuminate God's work in the world. Their collective good news is convincing and inspiring.

Stylistically, most of the stories end with the best part. This literary technique of not telling what happens after the baptism, for example, or when the promise is fulfilled subtly invites readers to find out for themselves. This book's emphasis on subjective experience means that the only way to find out the truth is to live it.

One:
FLEA MARKET SURPRISE

It was ninety-five degrees in the shade. It was even hotter than this as I worked outside in the bright Florida sun in August. Along with my partner, we were painting the massive exterior of a Spanish-style, two-story home. Even though we were spray painting the main body of the house, it was painting the windows and trim that seemed to take forever to do. This would be a two week job, and we would definitely add to the tans we had already accumulated.

My partner had gone into town for some supplies about noon time, when the maid called out and asked me if I would like to come in for lunch. This was a great treat, if for no other reason than to get out of the stifling heat for an hour.

As the maid, her daughter and I, sat down for a wholesome lunch and a cool drink, I asked if I could say a blessing. The mother gave me a definite "yes" as she was also a Christian. As we began to eat, we made small-talk for a while and I quickly found out that the daughter was not a Christian. My heart went out to her and I started to share my testimony, and then gave her the Good News of salvation through Jesus Christ. I shared with her how I was dying of a terminal disease several years earlier and how I gave my heart to Jesus. I told her how I was totally healed and the joy I now had in serving Him.

All the while I was witnessing to her daughter, her mother was cheering me on with her eyes! After finishing the witness and lunch, I thanked them for inviting me and went back out in the Florida heat. Somehow, it didn't seem so hot after I shared my faith. Sometimes after witnessing, I feel like I have been to an entire church service. This time was no different.

It was the following spring when I received one of the joyous surprises of my life! I took a Saturday off and went browsing in a large flea market in our city. It was huge and many thousands attended every weekend. I wasn't looking for anything in particular, so I was just kind of strolling along. I had been there about an hour, ambling along, when all of a sudden someone came up to me and hugged me and picked me up off the ground.

Before I could say anything, the girl said, "Remember me, remember me!" I thought for a moment, "Now where have I seen her?"

I didn't have time to say a thing. The girl loudly blurted out, "I am the one you witnessed to last summer and now I am saved!"

Oh boy, did we dance around and hug one another. I'm sure at least several people heard us and that was a witness in itself. And, there stood her mother with the biggest grin on her face. The mother and daughter thanked me profusely, and I thanked the Lord for allowing me to be a part of this precious one's journey to eternal life. I certainly received so much more than the previous summer of a lunch and air- conditioning.

We can experience great joy this side of heaven, being obedient and sharing His blessed Gospel!

> "Now he who plants and he who waters are one, and each will receive his own reward according to his own labor … " (Corinthians 3:8)

Two:
FROM A JEWEL TO A MORE PRECIOUS STONE

It had been a very difficult year, serving the Lord in a foreign country with my family of four. We had a customary stopover in Korea on our trip returning to America. I opted to remain in Korea for another two and half weeks, while my family traveled on to the United States. My destination was Seoul, Korea, and the famous Prayer Mountain, begun by Pastor Paul David Yonggi Cho. Cho now pastors the largest church in the world - a congregation of nearly one million. Along with my bags, I brought an electronic musical instrument which played beautiful songs to the Lord.

I checked into the small motel on Prayer Mountain. I was hopeful I would receive refreshment, restoration and healing from some deep hurts received while in ministry. A short time after I arrived, I started playing my instrument, just strumming some chords and singing to the Lord. I was amazed that, in a little over an hour, while ministering to the Lord, He gave me four beautiful praise songs. More importantly, while singing, tears welled up within me as the Lord brought to my mind those who had hurt me deeply. I forgave them and released them from my heart. Tears gushed from my eyes, down onto the instrument of praise, so much so, that I thought I would short it out!

After such a powerful cleansing by the Holy Spirit, I felt as if I were brand new again. However, there was a lingering question in me - "how do I stay cleansed and protected from deep hurt?" Jesus said, in Matthew 18:7, "Offenses will come," but He also said, "Don't take offense." What could happen inside me that would make me strong enough to withstand the many hurts and disappointments that come from ministry?

Well, the Lord directed me to start a study on "who He calls me," and "what I really am because of my position in Christ." With a pretty thorough knowledge of the Word, I began to find out fairly quickly "who" He calls His sons and daughters, those who are born-again. I found such precious and powerful words and phrases, as: "Beloved", "Holy", "Children of God", "Valued by God", and "Adopted."

All in all, I found thirty words and phrases describing "who" we really are in Christ. It affirmed, even more, the truth of God's Word about me, "Those who are born of the Spirit are spirit." I am really a spirit being. I wrote these down, eventually in alphabetical order. I sensed, though, it was not enough to just study these, but I needed to ask my Heavenly Father to really reveal these wonderful truths to me. The prayer went something like this:

"Father, thank you that you call me 'Beloved' and that is who I really am. Lord, reveal these truths about me, so I can live out who I really am to the fullest, and honor you."

I put these down on paper with the prayer, typed them up and made copies. I knew deep within me I was becoming stronger in the Lord, and was able to praise Him that much more because of His mighty work on the cross, not only taking away my sin and sinfulness, but making me somebody of great value to Him (Psalm 113).

After two and half weeks on Prayer Mountain, I was on a plane bound for the United States. I arrived in my hometown and stayed there for several days. I joined my family a few days later in a city 500 miles away, where a great revival was talking place. My family and I found ourselves staying nearly the entire summer in this city after a gracious Christian lady offered to let us stay in her home. Having been there for a week or so, I perceived that our hostess had a bad self-image. She had been saved fifteen years, and had participated in the revival in her church there for five years, but still could not shake an image of herself as being no good and unworthy. I knew in my heart, I was supposed to help her come to the reality of "who" she was in Christ.

So, I asked her, if I could help her and she immediately said,

"Yes!" I gave her the training module I received in Korea and asked her to thank the Lord for all He called her, which is who she really is in Christ. She did this for about two weeks in her devotional time. Jewel was desperate to break loose from the emotional and mental cage of her thoughts to be healed of a false identity she had

4

lived with for fifty-three years. Along with this desperation was a diligence to find out who she really was in the Lord, who had redeemed her.

On Friday, the 13th, no less, we came to her dining table to study God's Word. Right after I said a prayer, I started to say something when, with a startled look on her face, Jewel looked at me and said, "Oh Ed, I know how much God loves me! I know who I am in Christ!" Tears streamed down her face. Then, she got up and started dancing around her house. What a poignant moment for a teacher of the Word of God, to see the manifestation of a powerful truth of His Word become reality. Oh, what joy that day!

Several days later, Jewel came to me and said, "I have to see my mother. I don't want to see her. I don't really like her."

At that moment, I stopped her and said, "Jewel, what 'I' just spoke?"

She looked at me and grinned, and said, "The old 'I,' the old nature [before Christ]."

I said, "You, the new you in Christ can love your mother. The new person (2 Corinthians 5:17) is made to love her, and anyone else, unconditionally."

She just grinned and said she would go see her mother after she prayed and built-up her spirit to the things God said about her and who she really is in Him.

Yes, Jewel was saved for many years, but because she didn't know who she really was in Christ, she believed the lies spoken through her mother from the "father of lies" - Satan. Jewel can now live out to the fullest who she already is by doing the Word and seeing herself through the eyes of the Holy Spirit. By the way, Jewel's mother's words didn't penetrate her heart that day she visited her. The Word of God in Jewel's heart was just too strong for man's words!

> "And you shall know the truth, and the truth shall make you free" (John 8:32).

Three:
DOWN THE STREET CONNECTION

Has anyone ever come up to you and handed you an eleven hundred dollar check? Well someone did to me, in 1981. They felt the Lord wanted me to go on a mission's trip to a Far-Eastern country, so they supplied the full round-trip airfare. They said I would have to believe the Lord for my place to stay and my food. I could believe him for these, because He had already supplied the greater expense so what was it to supply the lesser? Being single, not having many expenses, I usually only worked about two weeks, or so, out of the month painting houses. I didn't have a lot of extra money, so I started praying for the funds that would be needed in several months.

I had a nice little apartment and, about once a week, I went down to the local laundry to do my wash. It was run by a Philippino family. The cleaning operation was really a family affair with older brothers, sisters, uncles and whoever working together.

One day, I just happened to mention I was going to their country and their eyes lit up. The first thing they said, without me saying another thing was, "You can stay with our father and mother! They live right in Manila. They would be glad to have you." Next, they asked where our evangelistic meetings would be held. I told them the Arenata Coliseum.

"Oh," they said, "our parents live only a few blocks from there!"

In fact, I found out it was about a ten-minute walk to the meetings. A gracious and loving family abundantly supplied my food and lodging during my stay. In a city of 8 million people, the Lord already had His reservations confirmed for me.

"The steps of a good man are ordered by the LORD"
(Psalm 37:26).

Four:
THE DOCTOR GETS A BIG RETURN

Dr. Steve Gyland has been a pediatrician for over forty years and is well- known over most of this large city where he and his wife practiced and lived. He has been the doctor for several generations of many of the same families. He and his wife, Rose, are also known for their Bible studies, personal testimony radio show and healing ministry. They are incredibly faithful Christians who just live and breathe the Lord Jesus wherever they go.

They have traveled around the world, witnessing, leading many to salvation, and ministering physical and emotional healing. Retirement from formal practice has not stopped Dr. Gyland and his wife. They still do their weekly radio show, and he is a medical examiner for a home health care service.

He and his wife have known a couple for over twenty years who served on the mission field for a while. One year, when the couple was on furlough, the Lord touched the Gylands heart to give them a donation of

$500.00 for their mission work. The very next day, the home health care service where Dr. Gyland works called and said they were raising his salary

$500.00 a month!

The directors of the home health care group didn't know about the donation, but the Lord surely did!

> "If thou sayest, Behold, we knew it not; doth not
> He that pondereth the heart consider it? and He that
> keepeth thy soul, doth not He know it? and shall not
> He render to every man according to his works?"
> (Proverbs 24:12)

Five:
AROUND THE WORLD BLESSING

My husband, Mark, had an overseas job that lasted six years. The first week we were in this developing country, my daughter and I visited the local orphanage. This is truly where my heart belonged, finding something of lasting value to do by assisting a facility that needed much help in every way. The first little girl I picked up we ended up foster-caring and then adopting a year later. My own daughter, Catherine and I would hold the babies, help feed them, change diapers and play with the toddlers. My husband would join us on the weekends, entertaining the little ones with his flute, dancing and playing games with them.

I was able to pray over the seriously ill babies and those who cried incessantly. Medical care, being what it was in this country, some of the babies died. I would hold one such child one day, and find out the next day that it hadn't made it through the night. It sure was tough going there, at times, but the Scripture in James 1:27 kept me going:

> " Pure and undefiled religion before God is this: to
> visit the orphans and widows in their trouble, and to
> keep oneself unspotted from the world."

My little daughter also gave me great consolation. She said, "Isn't it true that people live in heaven, live in hell or live on the earth?"

Amazed at this question from a five-year old, I answered, "Yes."

Her next question was, "Why do they call it dying?"

While I was thinking of an answer, she said, "Why don't we just call it moving."

I said, "Let's just do that." Oh, the blessed wisdom that is put in the hearts of children! This helped me so much in the days, weeks and years in this country as I faced the pain of seeing the needless deaths of babies.

Every summer for a vacation, we would go back to the States.

One year, we headed for Charlotte, North Carolina. We were going to a Christian seminar for several days of teaching. About three thousand people would be there. The first night we arrived, we were a little late and had to sit in the very back of a huge hotel ballroom. We happened to sit next to an American couple who had adopted a little girl of the same origin as our foreign country. We wanted to speak to them afterwards, find out where they had adopted their child, and share the same information with them.

Well, after the meeting everyone seemed to scatter, and we lost the couple in the crowd. The last day of the conference, our daughter's god- mother told us she had met the same couple and they wanted to meet us. As I said, there were about three-thousand people at the seminar, so the blessing we had of seeing them again was great. I asked them where they adopted their child and they said the name of our foreign city! The little girl was four-years old and we didn't recognize her. I next asked them for a baby picture of her to see if I had known her.

They showed us a baby picture, and I was taken aback, because I had prayed for this same baby several years ago. I had held this baby because she was crying so much, and prayed for peace and that she would be adopted by a Christian couple. The couple who adopted her were pastors from Ohio. Here I was, seeing the same child I had prayed for over three years earlier. And now, I was seeing her with her Christian parents halfway around the world! Isn't the Lord good to show us some of the fruits of our labor this side of heaven?

My tears of joy at that time more than made up for the tears of suffering for the little ones who "just moved."

> "For God is not unjust to forget your work and labor
> of love which you have shown toward His name, in
> that you have ministered to the saints, and do
> minister" (Hebrews 6:10 NKJV).

Six:
A WALK WITH JESUS

It seemed to me, the Lord wanted to do or say something to me that day. His voice came as a quiet but firm impression from my heart. I didn't know what to do next.

In my mind, I wanted to get on the floor, just to lay before the Lord allowing Him to just work in me, removing anything from my heart that would hinder my life with Him. In a little while, the Lord directed me to go into the bedroom and get on my knees without praying or saying anything. I immediately saw the feet of Jesus exactly as I had seen them twenty-five years before when Jesus took me above the clouds and I walked with Him. That vision was in about 1980. It was wonderful, and cannot be explained with human words.

In that vision, I was walking toward a door and I knew I would have to walk through that door to get into heaven.

Suddenly, I knew there was someone beside me. When I stopped walking I definitely knew it was Jesus walking step by step with me. I could see his feet with sandals and just the bottom of a gray robe at the height of His ankles.

Then we walked and walked, and in this experience, I felt like I never had any other life. I was just in the total present "presence" of Jesus. The love, joy and peace were indescribable - like nothing the world could offer. There are not words in the dictionary to describe what it was like. Suddenly, I was back in my chair at home. I fell on my knees on the floor and cried, begging God to take me back. God said, "Not now, Gladys, I need you there." In a few moments, the Lord said, "Keep these feet in your heart and mind." I responded, "I will keep these feet in my heart and mind forever."

In the last twenty-five years or so, with all the pulls and daily concerns of life, I had forgotten about this wonderful experience until recently. I am certain, without a doubt, these "feet" will take me where I should go and where I need to be for the Lord. I will follow the feet of Jesus!

"In Your Presence is fullness of joy" (Psalm 16:11b).

Author's Note: My wife and family, and I, have been the recipients of the benefits of much intercession and prayer by this dear sister for over 30years, even in some very dangerous situations. Our precious Intercessor is now eighty-five years old.

Seven:
A VERY SPECIAL WEDDING

Sally was the first person we longed to see whenever we entered the Ministry Office in Hong Kong. She always had a big smile and a big heart for people. We were teachers in a bordering country and we saw Sally several times a year, in our coming and going. We first met her in 1994, when we joined this overseas agency that assisted teachers with insurance and in-transit places to stay while on biannual visits to their place of residence.

Sally was the bookkeeper at this agency so we would check in with her about our financial matters. After we left the agency, several years later, we did not see Sally at all. Yet, from time to time we would ask about her.

In 2003, I received a call from one of my fellow church members saying that her brother was engaged to a girl who knew us.

"Who?" I asked.

She said, "Sally from Hong Kong."

I stood amazed by the phone for a couple of seconds. My friend told me that several years before, Sally had made it to a Bible School in West Florida, where she met and started dating my friend's brother. Later on, they were engaged and after graduating made their way to the East Coast of Florida to reside. They, in fact, had moved to our very city and wanted to see us. We were thrilled.

It had been about six years since we had seen Sally, so when we opened the door and she walked in, a flood of past memories filled our hearts. She looked so wonderful with that same beautiful smile and ever-streaming heart of joy! Her fiancé was a fine young man who clearly had a heart for God and devotion to Sally.

As our fellowship continued, they suddenly kind of turned to each other as if to say, "Should we ask him now?" I said, "What?"

Sally, kind of sheepishly, asked if I would perform their marriage ceremony. Oh, how honored and blessed I felt.

I gave a resounding, "Yes!" Being an ordained minister, I was licensed by the state of Florida to perform weddings et al. Here, sitting in front of us, was a blessed child of God whom we were so dearly fond of for years, being brought back into our lives in a very special way. We really didn't think we would see Sally until we all got to Heaven.

Now, she lives about seven miles from us with a wonderful husband and a one-year old baby boy. What a wondrous God we serve.

> " Delight yourself also in the Lord, And He will give
> you the desires of your heart" (Psalm 37:4)

Eight:
BETTER RETURN THAN THE MARKET

One summer when my wife and I were home resting from the mission field, we made a yearly visit to a small church that faithfully supported us every year. The pastor and his wife were very, very sweet people, always extending great kindness and consideration. On this particular Sunday, when we spoke, we noticed several new people in the congregation, especially one who led worship.

At the end of the service, the Pastor took up an offering for our work and we were so thankful for what we received, considering the size of the church. The Pastor and his wife invited us to lunch which we gladly accepted. As we were walking to the parking lot, the worship leader came up to us, quickly greeted us, and stuffed some rolled money in our hand. I put it in my pocket and we went on in and joined the others for lunch.

After lunch, we got in the car and headed for our temporary home. I had forgotten about the money the man gave me.

When I got home, I pulled the money out and it was six one-hundred dollar bills. It floored me. I quickly called the Pastor, got the guy's name and called and thanked him. He said he felt that was exactly what the Lord laid on his heart to bless us with.

It would be another two years before we were to see Steve. We were speaking at a different church and the Pastor was about to take up an offering.

All of a sudden the same man who gave us the $600.00 spoke up in the congregation and said several years ago he gave a certain amount of money ($600.00) and he was immediately blessed back with $2,700.00. We didn't know this before. Well, I guess his testimony increased the faith of some of the people at the present church as they blessed us with a good sized offering. The Lord has varied ways of blessing His people!

> "But this I say: He who sows sparingly will also reap sparingly, and he who sows bountifully will also reap bountifully" (2 Corinthians 9:6).

Nine:
A VOICE IN TIME

It was a beautiful day for riding bikes across the equally beautiful campus. My wife, I and our six-year old daughter did many fun things together, most of them simple activities where we could interact with one another.

We had to be creative and innovative to find fun things to do in this third world country where I worked. Sandy, my little girl, and I would often ride around the campus maneuvering around a man-made obstacle course created with strategically placed trees, bushes and hills. We would work our way in and out of the course with one, or the other, being the leader. The follower, for the moment, had to stay behind the leader and go exactly where the leader went. We had many fun times doing this.

One day we saw a huge paved hill which had a series of connecting paths leading down from an auditorium. We named it "our hill." The unique thing about the hill is that it had five zigzag sections to it so you had to watch your speed. You could get going fast, but you had to be careful. We had tremendous rides down the hill and delighted in each other's fun.

On this particular day, when all three of us were riding around campus, we suddenly came upon "our hill." I said to Sandy, "Let's go down our hill and show Mother how we can ride."

As we started off for the hill my usually quiet wife blurted out, "No!"

It startled Sandy and I, for we seldom heard Ann yell out so. We asked her why we couldn't ride down the hill and she said she heard the Lord say to her a resounding "No, don't go down the hill."

We promptly obeyed the Lord and went on riding on flat terrain. No more than a minute later, we found out the reason the Lord had told Ann "no." Sandy's chain snapped! It was a fairly new bike. Even so, the Lord knew that the chain would snap and Sandy could have been killed riding down the steep hill.

Oh, how our Heavenly Father takes care of us in all areas of our lives.

Truly, this was His voice in time!

"My sheep hear My voice, and I know them, and they follow me" (John 10:27).

Ten:
A MILLIONAIRE'S CONVERSION

Hi, my name is Barry.

I grew up in an upper-middle-class neighborhood in the late sixties. Close to my home was an upper-class section where I use to "hang" with the kids of these well-off folks.

By the time I was fourteen, I was hooked on alcohol. We would raid these same upper-class houses for every kind of booze imaginable when the occupants would go on vacation. When I was sixteen, the local law enforcement came to our school and conducted tests to see how much consumption each one of us partook of regularly. These questionnaires were given to us to be answered on a voluntary basis so I freely answered them. I was shocked when I found out I was a borderline alcoholic! Oh yeah, I did marijuana along with my drinking.

By the time I was twenty-five, I was very successful in the clothing business. I would buy slightly imperfect men's and women's fashions and sell them for a good profit.

Let's say "I bought by the inch and sold by the yard!"

During the next twenty-three years I had six retail outlets. I became a millionaire many times over. However, by the age of forty, I was so dependent on alcohol I would have delirium tremens. This scared me, so I tried to stop drinking, many times, only to pick up the bottle again.

My dependency on alcohol wrecked two marriages. With multiple DUI's (Driving Under the Influence) along with an offense for receiving stolen property, I ended up in jail awaiting a trial. I had money to bail myself out, but I wouldn't leave jail because I knew I would go right back to the alcohol.

In jail, I read the four gospels in the Bible over and over. The books of Matthew, Mark, Luke and John, which I kept repeatedly reading, showed me the love of Jesus Christ, how He died for me, and the way to His salvation. Oh, how reading the scriptures calmed me down! A wonderful peace settled over me.

I asked Jesus to forgive me of my sins and take over my life in the jail chapel. I spent a year in prison, where my mind was restored, as I withdrew from alcohol. I asked the judge, during my probation hearing, to put me in a Teen Challenge program I had heard about.

In January, 2004, I graduated from the rehabilitation program of Teen challenge. Six months later, I was given credentials to go back to the same prison to minister to the guys I served time with!

With alcohol, and drugs, I lost everything. But with Christ, I am rich in Him. My estranged twenty-year-old son located me through the Internet. Now he, along with my wife and daughters, ages ten and eight years old, are in daily telephone contact. The Lord has given me life itself, ETERNAL LIFE, and He is in the process of restoring all things. Thank you Jesus!

> "Though I walk in the midst of trouble You will revive me" (Psalm 138:7).

Eleven:
A CAR JUMPS OVER THE PASTOR

Riding to the church where I pastor, late that afternoon with my wife and oldest son, I had no idea that I would be part of the miraculous power of God to save us from a horrible crash. It all began when I noticed, through my rearview mirror, cars starting to scatter and pull off to the side of the road for some reason. I didn't hear an ambulance siren or see their warning lights, but I could tell something bizarre was going on behind me. Within a minute, I could clearly see a car moving wildly through the traffic, zigzagging in and out.

Instead of an ambulance, it was a car driving like an ambulance, but definitely not as carefully.

What did I do? I started praying! My wife, myself, and my son who was in the back seat prayed like never before. If this wild driver hit us, my son would be the first to take the hit. He was coming so fast I didn't have time to pull off the ride. As the car came up from behind us, all of a sudden it disappeared! Several seconds later, I saw the car come out over the top of us and land in a ditch. There was no way in the natural sense of things it could have gone airborne on its own. I believe with all my heart to this day an angel or angels lifted the car over us.

> " For He shall give His angels charge over you, to
> keep you in all your ways" (Psalm 91:11).

Twelve:
A LITTLE CHILD SHALL LEAD THEM

I have always said a prayer for my little girl, Angela, "Lord, use her for your glory." I started praying this when she was just about two years old. Sure enough, at about four, she started handing out Christian Salvation Tracts which explained to people how to receive Jesus as their Lord and Savior. After several years, she would join us on the mission field, living in a foreign land and being used in ways I never thought possible. The following is one such true story.

Our first year on the mission field was one of adjustment to a very different culture. The people were wonderful, hospitable and friendly. The food was delicious, but we always didn't know what we were eating, especially the meat. Actually, we lived on a large island off the mainland, so the air was quite refreshing. We had help in accomplishing many daily survival tasks that were a blessing, one of which was having a house helper, who would cook, clean and do the wash. This was an absolute necessity for us. Cooking three meals a day in this country is a time consuming task in which a person could spend all their time going to the market, chopping and preparing food, let alone the other household duties. Fortunately, we had a local native to help us. The only problem was she didn't know English at all. With a lot of hand signs and a bilingual dictionary, we did okay.

One day we were introduced to a university student who spoke some English reasonably well and she came several nights to prepare us some good dishes. We paid her the going rate and she did fix us some very good meals.

We are from the Deep South, but Jane fried up some pork chops for us like none I had ever tasted. Oh, I can still see and almost taste them. Oh, yes, it was real pork!

One day my little six-year old Angela had, what I believe, was a God- sent idea. The thought was, "Why not ask Jane if she wanted her to help with learning to speak and read English better?"

Jane readily agreed, because English is one of the best skills a native can learn since their country was opening up to business trade with the West. So, Angela proceeded to have an English lesson with Jane every time she came to help us. The only little twist to the lessons was Angela started off reading with her Children's Bible! The Word of God says to be "wise as a serpent and harmless as doves (Matthew 10:16)." Our little daughter knew the foreign student by reading the Bible. Faith would arise in her heart.

It wasn't too long after that, when Jane said she wanted to become a Christian. She sincerely prayed to ask Jesus to forgive her of her sins and be her Lord and Savior. What a joyous time that was.

She was our first convert in a country where religious activities are severely restricted and foreigners are forbidden to have any Christian influence with the local people. Our daughter was the main one to begin leading and bringing Jane to a decision for Christ. Jane was baptized in our big, deep bathtub and we were able to disciple her that year. She continued to be close to us until we left this country.

My prayers for Angela were that the Lord would use her, and keep giving her answers to her prayers. The Lord has used her to go on missions trips in Thailand, Costa Rica, and Scotland. Our continuing prayer for Angela is that she not only be a good moral Christian, but that she lives an exciting life of serving the Lord, every day, using her gifts to glorify His name and fulfill His purposes. He does answer prayer!

> "the child grew and became strong in spirit" (Luke 1:8).

Thirteen:
FORGIVENESS OVER   BREAKFAST

I can usually take or leave fast-food breakfasts. I usually leave them. There is something about sitting in your own little breakfast nook, with something hot to drink, and eating a variety of things, like eggs and bacon, or cereal. Just sitting there, enjoying drinking my morning coffee and seeing God's beautiful creation through the window, prepares me for the day.

This day, however, I was off and going at a pretty good pace when I decided to go to a local place for some breakfast. As I picked up my small tray with coffee and a biscuit, I turned to go into the little dining area to eat. I stopped suddenly, because I saw a man with whom I had a misunderstanding over some money he thought I owed him. He had done some work for me and I thought we had settled on a price, but he thought otherwise.

He didn't see me. I started to go and ask for a "to go" bag, but at that moment, I heard the Lord speak to me clearly, "Be not overcome with evil, but overcome evil with good."

When I heard Him say that, I proceeded ahead, not knowing if the brother would express his hurt and in turn try to hurt my heart. I just tried to be obedient to the Lord, believing that I could overcome any evil with good actions or words. As I approached his table, he looked at up me warily, but I immediately spoke up and asked him if I could join him.

He nodded a curt "yes," and I sat down. After asking how each other had been, we did address the matter at hand. Forgiveness came forth from both of us and we are good friends to this day. I am reminded of a Scripture that says, "The love of God is shed abroad in our hearts by the Holy Spirit" (Romans 5:5). I, as a Christian, had to choose the will of God to release His love that was already there. I didn't wait for feelings to come, but acted from love based on the desire and power of God's word. Another Scripture says, "love (God's love in us) never fails" (Romans 13:8) .

It sure didn't fail that day, and it will never fail in any situation as we appropriate it!

> "Be not overcome with evil, but overcome evil with good" (Romans 12:21).

Fourteen:
FIRST THINGS FIRST

It was a wonderful service, as usual, that Sunday morning! We glorified the Lord through beautiful praise and worship and heard a blessed message from the Lord through the pastor, who was preparing our hearts to serve the Lord with gladness for the upcoming week. About eight hundred believers were in this service, the usual number of those who attended each Sunday morning.

After the service, prayer was made available for people at the altar and quite a few people came forward. My wife and I, along with several others, were asked to stay and pray for people. The first lady who came up to us was in her late fifties. She wanted prayer for her hurting leg. As my wife and I laid hands on her to pray, I hesitated, because I wanted to hear the Lord's instruction on how to pray. Many times before, I would just pray for the obvious need out of my mind, but I had learned to hear God, the Holy Spirit, speak to my heart. Of course, the latter way was much more effective.

What I received from Him was a surprise! I heard the one word "unforgiveness" being spoken to my heart. Since the lady was almost 20 years older than me, I was reluctant to ask her if she had any unforgiveness toward anyone, but I had to be obedient to the Holy Spirit. The Lord won out over my natural tendencies, and I asked her if she had any unforgiveness toward anyone at all.

When I asked her, she immediately broke down and cried. She said, "Yes." She went on to tell us she was once engaged to be married. The man had jilted her and she had held bitterness in her heart for some time. I did not know this lady, and she was amazed at the fact that the Lord told me this. She experienced His great love and care for her through prayer that day. She wept profusely as she asked for forgiveness and was set free. The Lord certainly cared about her hurting leg, but he cared much more for the condition of her spiritual heart, the eternal part of her.

> " F or we do not look at the things which are seen,
> but at the things which are not seen. For the things

which are seen are temporary, but the things which are not seen are eternal" (2 Corinthians 4:18).

Fifteen:

I'VE ALREADY DONE THE GREATEST THING I CAN DO FOR YOU

Entering my little apartment that night, I had no idea that I would receive one of the greatest spiritual truths that would help carry me through many trials in the coming years.

As I stepped over the threshold of my two-room flat, I realized my rent was due the next day, on the first of the month. Being single and needing only about five hundred dollars to make ends meet each month, I only worked one job, painting a house per week in a month. I spent the rest of the time studying the Bible, going to Bible studies, or doing charity work. One day this would lead to attending Bible School and a fairly large ministry overseas. But right now, I needed rent money. I always tried to pay my bills on time and really never had any problem. I had some work coming up, but it didn't help me now.

As I walked on into my apartment, I talked with the Lord in a very simple, direct way. I said something not too profound like "Lord, I need help."

What He said next was incredibly profound and brought me great peace. He spoke in my heart these words: "I have already done the greatest thing I can do for you, and that is bringing you from spiritual darkness to spiritual light. What is it for me to do anything lesser?"

Oh, what a blessing to my heart! Imagine that. It says in Colossians 1:13, "He delivered us from the power of darkness and into the kingdom of the Son of His love. " (ASV Any spiritual act or transformation is surely greater than supplying rent money for a month. I felt such rest now, knowing somehow everything would be okay.

In a minute or two, I felt I remembered I should call home and talk with Mom or Dad, not to ask for the money, but just to see how they were doing. When I reached my folks, I asked how everyone was doing (I have two brothers and a sister), including my aunts and uncles. In the midst of the conversation, my mother asked if I had gotten the letter they sent me ten days ago.

I said, "No," so we verified my address. Since the address was okay, I told them I would check at the post office. When I hung up, a thought came to my mind to check the side door of my place, where I never entered or exited.

Well, when I opened the screen door there lay a letter from my parents and inside was a check from my Father that was more than enough to cover the monthly rent. Even though this wasn't an earth-shaking crisis, a heart- exploding truth had happened in me to show me that my Heavenly Father could take care of anything, because he had "already done the greatest thing."

> "Who hath delivered us from the power of darkness, and hath translated us into the kingdom of his dear Son:" (Colossians 1:13).

Sixteen:
THE WITCHDOCTOR AND THE ELDERLY LADY

There they went - thirty teens off on a Japanese 747 airline for Bangkok, Thailand, for a summer of reaching out to the lost with the Gospel of Jesus Christ. They were a part of an organization of 6,000 teenagers going to over thirty different nations around the globe. In the midst of them, was our precious thirteen-year-old daughter, Angela, heading out as if she were about to go on the biggest date of her life. In fact she, like all the others, was to have many dates and appointments with people who had never heard of the Lord Jesus.

Appointments would change their lives eternally. Our daughter and her team would be in Bangkok and the outlying villages for two months. They would live in dorms and share facilities with each other. Their activities would include street witnessing, dramas, and singing, all with seasoned interpreters. Angela, a trained dancer, like her mother, would use her skills in drama and dance to portray the Gospel. Others would speak. She was a good speaker on her own and could lead others to Jesus. Many Thai people would give their lives to the Lord that summer and over 100,000 thousand would receive Christ with all the teams around the world! Two incidents stand out which Angela feels demonstrate the love and power of the Living God.

One involved a witchdoctor in an outlying village. While the teens were sharing in the village, my daughter was asked to come over and share with the resident witchdoctor. After she had shared the Gospel with him, the witchdoctor received Christ. Angela went on to share with the witchdoctor that now, as a new-born believer in Christ, and as the person whom the villagers looked up to for guidance, he could have influence by The Holy Spirit and the way he lived his life out before them. He was so honored and receptive to what she shared. We know many lives have now been turned around through his sharing of the Gospel with his people.

Another incident took place on our daughter's last day of ministry. She was praying during her morning devotional time. The Lord gave her a picture, in her mind, of an elderly lady wearing certain clothes. The strange thing was she couldn't see her eyes. Angela was definitely touched by this vision and prayed for the lady. That afternoon, the team went to a nursing home and our daughter saw the exact same woman the Lord gave her in her devotional time.

She was amazed when she found out the woman was blind and, apparently, that is why she couldn't see her eyes. She went up to her and shared the love of Jesus Christ by His death on the cross for her. She led the woman to a saving knowledge of Jesus, and the woman was so thankful. The Lord said He would pour out of his Spirit in the last days and his servants would see visions and have dreams. He sure did this with this young handmaiden of His, and this elderly woman is destined for an eternal heaven with the living God!

> "And it shall come to pass in the last days, saith God, I will pour out of my Spirit upon all flesh: and your sons and your daughters shall prophesy, and your young men shall see visions, and your old men shall dream dreams..." (Acts 2:17)

Seventeen:
FROM EXECUTIONER TO LIVING FOR THE LIFE GIVER

He was one of the saddest-looking persons we had ever seen. His name was Mr. Ho, and he was brought to one of our Bible studies by Margaret, a native teacher, in the foreign land where we lived. About twenty people had gathered for our weekly meeting.

Margaret was faithful to bring new people to our home to share about the Lord. This time, she brought Mr. Ho, taxi driver she met when he took her home one night.

We had a very good meeting, as usual, with a good discussion period and prayer following the Bible study. This particular time, we opened the discussion up to talk about "death." We asked what the people thought about dying, and how they felt about loved ones who had passed away. When we came to Mr. Ho, he was very reluctant to talk about the subject, but finally opened up to us. He said he had been an executioner. He nearly cried when he said it. All of us were quite taken aback, as none of us had ever met someone who had executed people convicted for crimes.

Mr. Ho was not a Christian and he just didn't know how God could ever forgive him for executing someone. His face portrayed much guilt residing in his heart. He said he once shot an eighteen-year-old in the back of the head, execution style, with the young man kneeling down. This young man did not die right away, so Mr. Ho had to wait a good while until the fellow died. He said it was awful.

He quit this work as an executioner, probably because of the incredible stress. We asked him if he wanted to be free of this guilt forever and he said "yes."

We lead him in a prayer of salvation and a peace came over him. We asked Margaret to minister him using the verse, "There is now no condemnation to those who are in Christ Jesus. For the law of the Spirit of Life in Christ Jesus has freed us from the law of sin and death." This is found in Romans 8:1-2.

She was faithful to minister it to him.

The next week, the precious Christians gathered. After an opening prayer, we greeted one another. My wife and I noticed a man we had never seen before, and we asked each other who he was. We asked Margaret, and she said it was Mr. Ho! His face had been so transformed by the power of God working in his heart, that we didn't even recognize him. His eyes were glowing with the presence of the living God in him. What a blessed, dramatic transformation.

The old Mr. Ho was dead (See 2 Corinthians 5:17) and the new Mr. Ho emerged!

> " Unless a man be born-again he cannot see the kingdom of heaven" (John 3:3).

Eighteen:
GOD KNOWS THE HEART

Prisons can be a bittersweet place to share your faith. On the one hand, many inmates because of their circumstances are very open to listen to you. On the other hand, the lives of those incarcerated have had many years of trouble and heartache leading up to their crime and punishment, and just want to get out of their cell. Many, of course, are weary of anyone telling them anything, as they have been conned and have conned and lied to others for so many years that their heart is not always open to you or the Lord. But my wife and I, knowing the power of the Word of God and the Holy Spirit as we minister, just try to be obedient and leave the results up to Him. We were asked to fill in for a minister who regularly taught at this particular institution.

We were to substitute for two weeks in a row at a women's prison on the outskirts of our city, teaching about an hour in the Word of God, and then offering an invitation to receive Jesus as Lord and Savior. We always looked forward to sharing the Word of God, even with one person, but this night we would have about 40 women attending. I have forgotten the message the Lord put on my heart those many years ago, but it was the invitation and the following prayer I will never forget.

When I gave the invitation to receive Jesus, several came forward, and it was such a joy to pray with them for a brand new life, starting from the inside out. When I got to one girl, named Julie, she seemed very beaten down by her past and she could hardly look at my wife and me.

As we prayed for her and tried to hear the Holy Spirit, I heard one word "abuse." I asked Julie, out of the hearing of anyone else, if she had ever been abused in any way. She broke down and cried buckets of tears. I laid hands on her and told her that Jesus wanted to take all of the years of pain and suffering from her. She nodded and kept on crying deep down within. She received a Bible and we told her we would see her the next week.

The following week, we met at the same time and about the same number of people came. In walked Julie, and her face had been transformed to one of beauty instead of holding the mental and emotional scars of many years. It was a transformation that only the living God can do. I almost didn't recognize her. Women talk about having makeovers. Well, this is one makeover that can't be compared to any physical makeover, ever. She sat down and was reading her Bible, and it was the picture of one reading a love letter that was touching the heart in its deepest recesses.

Her eyes were glowing with "Who" was now living in her heart. She opened up her heart to the greatest lover of her soul that she could ever have

- The Lord Jesus Christ. Even though she was incarcerated physically, she was set free in her spirit and soul.

> " The light of the body is the eye: if therefore thine eye be single, thy whole body shall be full of light" (Matthew 6:22).

Nineteen:
HE COULDN'T SPEAK

Oh, what a hot night it was, when I arrived at the outdoor church in the Philippines in 1980. An outdoor church in the tropics is one in which there is only a tin roof covering to provide protection from the rain and sun. It was around seven p.m. when I arrived, with the meeting scheduled to start at eight p.m., I thought I would pray for one hour.

As I walked into an outside office built onto the church, I could already feel the presence of God. I quickly found out people had been praying all through the night before, and the next day, to prepare the place for a mighty move of God. The people of the Philippines and most countries in the Far East will stay for hours praying, listening to sermons and being in the Presence of God.

On that night, I preached about one hour and thirty minutes, the Lord building faith in the hearts of the people to receive salvation, healing and deliverance. At the conclusion of the preaching, I noticed a group of upper- teen and early-twenties people sitting to my right side against a little barrier. They had been brought there to receive Jesus as Savior - they were known drug addicts. Every one of them received Jesus and was dramatically touched. Many others were saved that night.

After people received salvation, I called for those who wanted to be filled with the Holy Spirit. So many came forward that I lined them up in rows because I was going to lay hands on them. When I started praying and laying hands on people, a startling thing happened. It was something I had never experienced. Before I could lay hands on people, they started falling all around me, so much so that I had to get out of the way and just let the presence of the Lord have His way.

A few minutes after the supernatural intervention of God happened, people started calling out to me and running up to me. They literally shouted for me to come over to a certain man lying on the ground, under the power of God. When I got to the man, who was about 35 years old, he was praising God. His countenance was exuberant. I was told that the man was born dumb. He hadn't spoken a word in all of his thirty-five years, and yet, the first words out of his mouth were glorious praises!!! This man was so eager to get healed that he came up for the time of the filling of the Holy Spirit. The Spirit of the Lord filled him so much that a miracle took place.

> "And great multitudes came unto him, having with them those that were lame, blind, dumb, maimed, and many others, and cast them down at Jesus' feet; and he healed them:" (Matthew 15:30)

Twenty:
BLESSING FROM THE GROSS

The season in my life was a time of stretching. However, I didn't want to be stretched! As a newly divorced single mother making house payments, learning to make new decisions and fulfilling all the responsibilities my ex- husband had assumed was a new and scary place to be in for me. The financial strain was ever-consuming. For that reason, in the natural, it made no sense when the Lord spoke to me one Sunday saying I was to be stretched even further.

I was sitting in church writing out the tithe check, which I did faithfully every payday. The Lord spoke to me, and said to tithe off my gross income and not my net. I already felt my gross salary was "gross!" How could a loving Father God ask something so ridiculous of me? The new school year was about to start and I had to purchase new clothes and school supplies for my son. My former husband was faithful in his child support payments, but my son was in a private Christian school due to the undesirable situations in the local public school. His tuition costs and food consumed the whole child support payment.

Sitting in my seat, I struggled with whether or not to obey the quiet voice I felt speaking to my spirit. I rationalized that if I didn't obey the leading of the Lord I would not experience peace in my life about this situation. I made the decision. With renewed confidence, I had made the right choice, and I tithed off of my "gross" gross!

Later in the day, my ex-husband came over with my son who had been spending the weekend with his father. I was shocked when they came in the door with bags and bags of new school clothes and all the supplies he needed for the year! The only thing they had not purchased was a winter coat.

When it came time to write out my tithe check a month later, I started wavering because of the need to purchase the jacket. Once again, I heard the quiet voice "Tithe off your gross, I will supply the jacket today after church."

Once a year, our parish had a swap day where we would bring in our good used clothing and took what we needed in exchange. I just knew the jacket would be there! After the service, I walked over to the table where the clothes in my son's size were displayed. There was no jacket.

I waited around watching for the person to bring the jacket. No jacket. Finally, after all the clothes were cleared away and tables taken down, a woman rushed out of the sanctuary over to the clothes area. She looked in dismay because everything was gone. She said she had something in her car to contribute and ran to her car. I was the only one still standing there. There was a huge beaming smile on my face when she handed me the only item she had brought, a brand new jacket in my son's size! Not only did I wear a huge smile that day, but the rest of my days, I wore expectancy in my heart regarding the faithfulness of my Heavenly Father.

> "Bring all the tithes into the storehouse, that there be food in My house, and try me now in this, says the Lord of Hosts, if I will not open the windows of heaven" (Malachi 3:10).

Twenty-One:
BACK-ALLEY DELIVERANCE

As I write this, I can remember the exact wild night this event took place.

It was the night before Thanksgiving, and President Reagan was about to finish his first year in office. At the time, I had a house ministry in a lower- middle class neighborhood of our city. I had been fasting and praying for two weeks almost to the day, as directed by the Lord. Usually, there is a very definite reason for fasting so long, but this time, I didn't know the reason, but I was soon to find out.

We had gone to bed about 10:00 p.m., that night before Thanksgiving Day. I was in a sound sleep until I was awakened about 2:00 a.m. by some frantic screaming. As if rehearsed, I immediately called for another Christian brother in the other room and told him to hurry and come because someone was in trouble. We ran down the stairs of our second-story apartment and headed for the screaming. It was coming from the alley behind our house. When we got to the scene, a big, strong guy was hitting a twenty-something year old girl with what we called a "ghetto blaster"- a very large cassette tape player and radio.

Instantly, again as if it was rehearsed, I told Mike to get the girl down the street to another sister's house, which he did. The big guy now turned on little me!

His arms were almost as big as my head and they magnified themselves through his tight tee shirt. He was about ten feet from me when he swiveled around and took a step towards me.

In an instant, I said, in a loud commanding voice, "In the name of Jesus, I command you to stop!" He stopped on a dime and didn't move. Some would call this surreal. I knew it was the supernatural power of God working through me to stop the demonic force driving this man. I knew now that the two weeks of fasting and prayer had prepared me for this moment in time.

The man settled down and shared with me how he had lost his

job as an air-traffic controller when he wouldn't go off strike. This made him very upset and "something came over him" and he got into an argument with his girlfriend. As I shared the Lord with him, he listened intently. I strongly encouraged him to give his life to Jesus. He said he would consider it.

The man could have torn off my head with his bare hands, but his natural power was no match for the SUPER-natural power of the Lord Jesus Christ. By the way, the girl was a born-again believer who got involved with this unbeliever. She was unequally yoked (2 Corinthians 6:14), but the Lord in His mercy and grace delivered her out of the hands of death. She really could have lost her life. A little inconvenience of fasting and prayer was a small price to pay for the life of a child of God.

That day the Lord released me from the fast and I had a very sumptuous feast on Thanksgiving Day with much to be thankful for!

> "For He has delivered us out of the power of darkness into the kingdom of the Son He loves" (Colossians 1:13).

Twenty-Two:
FLOATING OUT TO SEA

Driving to the beach with my son that holiday weekend of July 6, 1977, I had no idea it was a day that would change my life forever. The events of that day were so unbelievable, that I only shared a portion of this story for several years. Not until I came to a place in my walk with God where I could serve Jesus Christ with abandonment, was I able to freely share the full story.

It all began when my friend, Tommy, invited my son, Chris, and myself to the beach to celebrate the Fourth of July with him and his family at a hotel at Jacksonville Beach, Florida. Tommy's grandmother lived next door to me when I was growing up, so Tommy and I were close, like a brother and sister.

Tommy had also invited my husband to the outing, but he wanted to stay at home.

Tommy and I were having a wonderful time in the water with Chris, who was five years old, and Tommy's cousin, Shelly, who was Chris's age. Shelly and I were in inner tubes, and Chris was hanging between my legs. The sea started getting a little rough, and I started drifting away from Tommy and Shelly. I was drifting in the opposite direction. Florida often has storms that come up quickly, and that is just what happened. The waves started crashing violently. I don't remember whether I jumped off the inner tube to get back to shore or if the waves knocked me off. What I do remember, is that they were crashing over our heads.

I put Chris on my shoulders. I was underwater, but the next wave knocked Chris off. He was reaching out to me to save him and I was reaching back, but our fingers were an inch apart from meeting one another. The waves started pulling Chris under, while it pushed me to the crest, and then we reversed positions. Chris had recently taught himself to swim. Sizing up the situation, he started swimming parallel to the shore toward Tommy.

He reached Tommy, but in his panic, started pulling Tommy underwater. Tommy was already in a weakened condition, because he was recovering from a recent cancer surgery. My best friend, my son, and I (who couldn't swim) were drowning. Five-year old Shelly, still on her inner tube, was floating out to sea. Her mother left her eighteen-month-old twin brothers alone on the beach to swim out to help her.

In desperation, I yelled out, "God save me!"

As soon as I yelled, something hard hit me in my side. A surfer came up, from the opposite direction of where I was looking and pulled me on his surfboard.

I kept begging him to take me to my son, but, instead, he took me towards the shore.

He told me we were in a dangerous run-out and pushed me off the surfboard where the waves were breaking at my waist. The undertow was so strong! I still couldn't get to shore. We were in-between two life guards, who never left their stands. In the craziness of the moment, when I couldn't get to shore, I went back out to my son. Another surfer came up and helped Shelly who was still on the inner tube. I got to Tommy and Chris after the first surfer reached them, (I don't even remember how I got there). The other surfer brought Shelly and her mother to us. Between Shelly's inner tube and the two surfboards, we all managed to get to shore.

I was weak and trembling when I looked at the surfer who rescued me. I was scared because, as I looked at him, I thought I was looking at Jesus Christ! He had the kindest eyes and dark brown shoulder-length hair with a short beard. I was so in awe that I stuttered as I asked his name. I gave a big sigh of relief when he told me his name was Gary! I knew how I had been living, and believe me, Jesus Christ was not a part of it! Tommy's parents had seen all of the action from their hotel room and came running down to the beach.

Just after I asked Gary his name, they rushed up, and asked if I was OK. I told them, "yes," and turned to thank Gary. Within that twenty seconds, both surfers had disappeared from the beach. People just don't disappear on a beach! They had to be angels!

God REALLY got my attention that day! I decided either I was

41

so awful God didn't want me, or He had big plans for my life. When I called out to God, I was calling out for Him to save me out of my near-fatal situation. Instead of just physical rescue, He came and gave me an eternal, blessed life as well!

As I grew in my love for Jesus Christ, and started surrounding myself with believers, I began sharing my "angel" experience. I thought people would think I was crazy. Now, I know I was crazy not to believe in a loving Savior and His angels.

> "for this my son was dead and is alive again; he was lost and is' found.' And they began to be merry" (Luke 15:24 NKJV).

Twenty-Three:
GOD HAS CRUISE CONTROL

After twenty years of marriage, one of the desires of my heart was to take my precious wife on a cruise to the Caribbean.

I had lived in the islands for a while, and so wanted her to experience the incredible beauty of these dots in the ocean, and that "laid back, don't-have- anything-to-do" feeling on the deck of a ship.

There she was, Ellen, my wife, lounging in a deck chair with one of her historical novels. She couldn't have looked more relaxed, and consequently, I just didn't want to bother her. I walked around the large cruise liner, meeting people, and enjoying the sun and breeze bathing my face and arms. After an hour or so, I ambled back to where Ellen was reclining. She was just staring out at the sea so I sat down beside her. In a few minutes, we were chatting with a couple and telling them how we had become Christians. When they left, an older man, and one who looked like his son, came up and greeted us. They overheard us talking about our Christianity and told us they were also Christians.

Paul, the son, related to us how he had suffered with the tormenting condition of hives. He had overheard me tell the other couple how I had been instantly healed by God of an incurable disease and asked me to pray for him.

Ordinarily, we would have prayed for him right there on the deck, but I felt led to tell him we would wait on the Lord and see how He would have us pray.

The noisy, windy conditions at the moment were not the best time to hear the Lord. We asked for Paul's cabin number and said we would get in touch with him shortly. We were diligently trying to hear the Lord and what He would have us pray. We've learned over the years not to just say a quick prayer, but wait to see if there were any blockages to healing, like a broken- heart or known sin in a person's heart. Not to say everyone who remains unhealed has known sin, but blockages sure can occur.

Well, the next day we ran into Paul, with his dad in the ship's store. He asked me if we had heard anything from the Lord. My wife told him the Lord had showed her the hives were due to a fear he was facing. She told him he was fearful that a sin he had committed, years earlier, would be found out. This was causing the hives. Paul confessed that what she had told him was true, and related the matter.

He and I decided then, we would meet with my wife an hour later, and in the meantime, we would go work-out in the ship's gym. As Paul and I were exercising, he said to me, "The Lord seems to be telling me that my faith will make me whole." At that moment, a scripture flooded my mind. Jesus said, in Mark 10:52, "Go, your faith has made you whole."

So I said to Paul, "Go, your faith has made you whole." So Paul left, and we did not meet with my wife for prayer. I knew this was the Spirit of God speaking to us because of the way it came smoothly from my heart. The next morning, we were awakened at six-thirty a.m. by the phone and Paul was on the line yelling out, "I'm healed, I'm healed." The Lord healed him after suffering from this condition for many years. Praise the Lord! Paul received a very unexpected, but much-desired benefit on this cruise.

> "But Jesus turned him about, and when he saw her, he said, 'Daughter, be of good comfort; thy faith hath made thee whole.' And the woman was made whole from that hour" (Matthew 9:22).

Twenty-Four:
GOD USES ATHEISTS

There we were sailing out of one of the most beautiful harbors in the world, starting on an adventure of mission and orphanage work. We found ourselves at the outset of the journey on the back of the liner. We were on an upper deck and our little girl went down on a lower deck, ever under our watchful eyes. Soon, Debby was talking with an older couple and they seemed to be having a good time.

In a little while we saw her walking toward us with the couple. We met the couple and immediately seemed to have an instant connection. He was a businessman who had some building projects going on in the city where we were headed. They invited us to dinner that night on the ship, and we were glad to go with someone who spoke English, and knew the food we should eat in this foreign land.

On arriving at dinner, we noticed one of the ship's officers. He was introduced to us as Chief Officer of the ship. We had a delightful night, eating the right food, and not partaking of any alcohol offered to us. Before we said, "Goodnight", the Officer offered to take all our bags down through the hole of the ship the next morning, thus avoiding the crowd of disembarking passengers.

Walking back to our stateroom, I casually said to my wife not to expect anyone to come and pick up our bags, as all the men, besides us, were close to being drunk. But, sure enough at seven a.m., we heard a knock at the door and the officers were there to take our bags. We were a little unnerved at this time, for we had stuck about eighty pieces of Bible material throughout our bags. We had arrived in a country that taught Atheism, and since these men were Communist officials, we were full of joy when we made it right through Customs with little trouble. The officials had no idea how they were helping God's people to bring in His message of truth and love and salvation through Jesus Christ. This would be the first of many open doors and God's favor we would experience as we entered this land for the Lord.

> " I know your works. See, I have set before you an open door, and no one can shut it..." (Revelations 3:8).

Twenty-Five:
GRAND REUNION

The last time I saw my daughter, Heidi, was when she was just a year and a half old. That was over twenty years ago and she is now twenty one. All of those years, I never thought I would ever get to see Heidi again, even to the point that I totally gave up looking for her.

However, last year in September, my brother, who is into genealogy, was searching the Internet for relatives from the past and came across an email dated, January 5, 2001. The email was from my daughter who was looking for me. When I read the email I broke down and cried. I then knew the Lord wanted me to find her after all these years. I sent a letter to her email address, but it was returned stating "no such address". My brother then offered to pay for an Internet search detective to see if they could find out anything.

They sent back a known address, and I sent a certified letter to that address. The letter was sent back to me stating that no one lived there. This took place on October 20. I did not get discouraged, but kept up my faith and prayers. I knew in my heart, God wanted me to find my daughter or I never would have seen the email she sent looking for me. I was praying somehow the Lord would bring us together but, as of yet, with no results.

I was talking with one of the ladies at church, and she said I should ask the Lord to show me how to find her. Well, I started praying that way. I then received an email from my brother suggesting I should put an ad in the local paper (Oregonian) in Portland, Oregon, where I believed she lived. I live in Florida. In December, I put the ad in the paper which would only run for just ten days. The way the Oregonian worded the ad was as follows:

IF ANYONE KNOWS THE WHEREABOUTS OF
HEIDI ANN -DRESSLER, 7/28/78, IN
PORTLAND, OREGON, PLEASE CALL 904-725-
5542, COLLECT.

About the same time, in late December, 2001, my pastor had

asked at the end of the year, that the head of each household pray the blessing of God over their family. Those who were single, would write them down on paper, and have the Elders of the church pray over them. I had three blessings to be prayed, but the first and foremost one was that my daughter, Heidi and I would be reunited.

The ad ran its course with no results. A few weeks later, on January 14, 2002, a year after my daughter sent the email looking for me, I had a call from a lady.

She said, "I saw an ad in the paper that said, 'if anyone knows where Heidi Ann Olson-Dressler is to call this number,' is that right?"

I said, "Yes, it is. Who is this?" She said, "This is Heidi."

I was standing at the time; when I heard this, I fell back into my chair. I stuttered and said, "Do you know who this is?"

She said, "No, I don't know who this is."

I told her, "I am your father, Dale Dressler."

We both began to cry for about five minutes. I couldn't believe it! For over twenty years, I never thought I would ever see my daughter, Heidi, again, even to the point of giving up all hope. Only God, alone, could have done this and to Him goes all the glory and honor. That night, we talked for about two and a half hours. On February 22, 2002, I was finally able to see my twenty-three year old daughter who was only a little over a year old when I last saw her.

Praise be to the Lord God Jehovah!!! What a day of rejoicing it was.

> " And He will turn the hearts of the fathers to the children and the hearts of the children to their fathers " (Malachi 4:6).

Twenty-Six:
THE LIFTER OF MY HEAD

It sure was a sweet fellowship Gary and his wife, Chrissy, and I had that night. They were one of several married friends of mine. I, as a single guy, would visit on a regular basis. As Christians, we had some good, clean fun sharing about our daily activities and centering a lot of our conversation around our Savior and hero Jesus. I was so blessed in having this precious couple, as close friends that I was honored when I was asked to be the substitute "Father of the Bride," giving Chrissy away at her wedding , because her parents lived in Hawaii and couldn't make it to the blessed event. It was a beautiful ceremony outside in a park. With my participation in the wedding, to a degree, brought us into a closer relationship relative to the short time we had known one another.

I'll never forget the prayer and song we had this particular night. It was just a natural thing for us to do and we finished off the night with an up tempo song, "The Glory and Lifter of my Head." Some of the other words were: "for thou O Lord art a shield for me, the glory and lifter of my head."

I didn't know how these words would play such an important part in saving my life in only a few minutes after they were sung.

Later, as I swung my little Volkswagen Beetle out of their driveway, I still had the catchy tune in my head. I was actually singing it as I approached the red light just a block from my friends' house. Seeing the green light in the dark night ahead on this little-traveled street, I felt a peace about my recent visit and the song in my heart and mouth. Nearing the traffic light, all of sudden a flash of light from a speeding car on my left came into view. I had not been looking for any other car in this situation, but as I sang the song, "The glory and Lifter of My Head," my head was lifted to see the car. It was a big, long 1970's sedan.

If I had not stopped, on what seemed like" on a dime", I would not have been here today writing this story. With the speed and size of the car, and it being on my left side, I would have been directly plowed into. I would have been crushed. I believe with all my heart the Lord put this song in our heart to sing fifteen minutes before, and as I sang those words, He lifted my head to see in time to save my life!

> "He is the glory and the lifter of my head" (Psalm 3:3).

Twenty-Seven:
A LAWYER'S CONVERSION

We have all heard the lawyer's jokes, but this true story is no joke. My older brother, Roger, who is now a state judge, started out as a lawyer. My father, who had also been a state judge, knew many people in the city we grew up in, which assisted my brother in starting with good name recognition when he began his law practice. He practiced law for many years before becoming a judge himself. In his early years, with hard work, he developed a good law firm with some fine lawyers.

I had moved away from our city to go to college, and had continued to live away from my home town for a while. I was surprised, when I came back to the city for a visit, to see my brother had an office on the top floor of the tallest building in the city. A beautiful reception room, many nicely decorated meeting rooms, and a large law library with gorgeous wood paneling made for a nice working environment.

I was proud of my brother in many ways. He had become a Christian and had overcome a major drinking problem. Then he began helping many others, which continued for years, to overcome their addictions. I had also become a born-again Christian, several years before, and my life was making a difference in other people's lives.

My gifting, was sharing the Gospel of Jesus Christ in a very gentle, yet straightforward manner, clearly presenting the Good News. I look for opportunities, wherever I go, to plant a seed of the Gospel here or there or share my testimony and the plan of salvation.

One day, as I visited my brother at his office, he had to go out for a while so I sat around the office waiting. While I was waiting, I ran into my brother's law partner, Stan. He was a very likable guy, friendly as always, sincerely asking how things were going in my life and with my family. He had a break in his time, and he asked me to step into the law library so he could catch up on what had been happening with me.

I hadn't seen Stan since I became a Christian so I started there. I told him about how Jesus had healed me of great bitterness in my heart when I gave my life to the Lord. I also told about my physical healing of a terminal disease through prayer. I related how I had gone to Bible school and was doing part-time Christian ministry.

He thought that this was just fascinating and was so happy for me. Of course, with my testimony I shared the Gospel. At the time, Stan was about forty-five years old, and was not part of any church. He had a beautiful wife, a good marriage, fine sons and daughters, plenty of money and he was in excellent health.

By all standards, he really didn't have the usual problems that lead prosperous Americans to a saving knowledge of Jesus Christ. We chatted for a few more minutes and then I met with my brother.

I started praying for Stan and his family. When the Lord leads me to witness to someone, I know I must begin to pray for them because the Lord has started drawing them to Himself. It was about six months later, when I received a call from my brother.

He said Stan had called him at two a.m. that morning and yelled out to him, "I know how much Jesus loves me!"

Stan had become a Christian. He, his wife and family, and his mother and father they were now attending church. One man's life affected so many. Stan had no real great need in the natural sense of things, but the Lord sure reached him with the need all of us have, that of eternal salvation!

I have seen Stan several times since his salvation and he is serving the Lord with gladness and fervency. I am so thankful that I didn't look at Stan from his natural condition, but saw him as a very nice, hard-working man who still needed salvation. Yes, and a lawyer at that!

> "For My thoughts are not your thoughts, nor are your
> ways my ways, says the Lord" (Isaiah 55:8).

Twenty-Eight:
A BABY'S HEALING

My time of carrying Nathan was a blessing but the first sign of concern was at the on-start of labor. When I was about to deliver, my midwife noticed my baby's heart beat was really fast. She listened for a long time. When the heart rate remained fast, she urged Ted, my husband, and I to go to the hospital. We started praying right away. After a few minutes the heart rate was normal and our beautiful, eight pound Nathan came forth.

When Nathan was about 6 weeks old, he became sick. He was hardly eating and just wasn't acting himself, so off to the doctor we went. I told our doctor of all the symptoms - not eating and not wetting his diaper. She diagnosed him with Thrush and gave us a prescription.

The next day, he was worse and was becoming lethargic. We returned to the doctor's office and then rushed him, by ambulance, to the hospital. Nathan was put on oxygen.

After waiting for hours in the emergency room, the doctors came in and told us our baby was very sick. A man in the Emergency Room asked if my baby would be all right. I blurted out, "Yes, we serve an awesome God."

Finally, in a few hours, Nathan was sent to the Pediatric Intensive Care Unit. When we went into his room, our little guy was hooked up to a feeding tube with about ten I.V.'s, an oxygen tube, and a heart monitor. He looked in bad shape.

The doctors finally diagnosed him with Walffe Parkinson's White Syndrome. They also said he had a mass on his heart. The WPW Syndrome was not that serious, but the doctors were very concerned about the mass on his heart.

We began praying and praying and praying. We posted Bible scriptures around his bed and room. We also had praise music playing 24 hours and, we sat around quoting healing Scripture to him. The doctors said he would most likely have brain and organ damage. We believed that he would breathe on his own. He did. We believed they would take out the feeding tube. They did. We believed he would have no brain damage. He didn't. Nathan finally came home with only one prescription to take for the WPW to keep his heart in control.

One month later, we ended up back in the hospital because the medicine wasn't doing its job. After a week in the hospital with Nathan on stronger drugs, we went home. Our precious boy was on one medicine twice a day, and another prescription three times a day. As we continued to pray, praise and thank God, Nathan was off all medications after six months. He was totally healed. God is so good!

I have seen the doctors since Nathan's healing. They said it was quite a struggle just to keep Nathan alive. I thank the Lord for the skill of the doctors and the medicine that was available to us, but we definitely needed the Lord's intervention many times through this crisis.

> "If you can believe, all things are possible to him who believes" (Mark 9:23).

Twenty-Nine:
IT ALL CAME OUT IN THE WASH

What a wet day it was. Not because of any rain - there wasn't any. I had been pressure washing the outside of a church, and the over-spray was soaking me as much as a good Saturday night bath. I had contracted to paint the interior of the church, paint the steeple and wash the exterior of the church. After I finished washing the church, I started on the front-entrance walks.

As I walked to the front sidewalk, from the center walk, I noticed a drawing right in front of the Church. To my amazement, as I washed this particular square of the walk, I slowly saw unfold a drawing of a pentagram - a five pointed star with a circle around it. This is a common figure used in witchcraft and devil worship.

I started praying out of my spirit and stood against any curse that was placed on the church. The church had a recent history of a pastor who just up and left and a series of strange noises during the day when the new pastor was there - doors opening and closing; weird wind noises; creaking sounds. I heard these myself, and I was the only one in the building.

The very next day, after I told the Pastor about the pentagram, he and the church members gathered around the square where it was located, and prayed in Jesus' name, nullifying any curses put on the church.

The strange noises suddenly stopped and a growth in the church membership started taking place. I pray often, "Lord command your light to shine out in the darkness."

He is so faithful to do this.

> " Behold, I give unto you power to tread on serpents
> and scorpions, and over all the power of the enemy:
> and nothing shall by any means harm you" (Luke
> 10:19).

Thirty:
HIS DEATH, THEIR LIFE

Robert was a forgotten boy by his parents. His father was just too consumed with his business to be any kind of father to him at all. His mother was caught up in enjoying the money her husband made in his successful work.

Robert did catch the attention of a teacher in his high school one day. She was not his teacher, but overheard one of his teachers say how bright Robert was, but that he lacked the motivation to study. Apparently from the lack of the love of his parents, he had fallen into rebellion and desired the attention and love of someone. This is where Margaret, the caring teacher, came into the picture.

Margaret invited Robert over to a Bible study my wife and I held in a third-world country where I was employed. When we first met Robert, he was very kind, but sad with no purpose in life. Since Margaret had related his family background to us before he came over, we reached out to him with extra special love. Our Bible studies usually lasted about one hour with some discussion and prayer afterwards. We gave Robert a New Testament and hoped he would come back. Little did we know how he was touched by the Lord in the meeting. Margaret said he went home and read the entire New Testament all the way through that night. Shortly afterwards he gave his heart to Jesus and became a born-again Christian.

The next time we saw him, his whole countenance had changed because he had found the greatest love anyone could find - the unconditional love of God. His grades changed for the better, as did his relationships with his teachers and classmates. He changed so much that some of his classmates started attending the meetings with Robert. When it came time to go home for our summer break, we knew Robert would be in good hands with Margaret as she continued to show Christ's love and care through discipleship.

It was at the end of our summer vacation we received the news from our overseas country, through Margaret, that during the summer Robert had tried to break up a fight between some youths.

When a truck load of soldiers arrived, they began swinging clubs. Robert, although innocent, was clubbed to death by the soldiers. Of course, his classmates were deeply grieved over his death.

During their grief many of his classmates had dreams of Robert dressed in white ascending up into the sky. Many of them gave their life to Jesus because of this young man's life and death and ensuing dream. A life that seemed to be going nowhere is completely turned around, and his temporary life on this earth helped others gain eternal life. To God be the glory, great things he has done!

> "And we know that all things work together for good
> to those who love God, to those who are the called
> according to His purpose" (Romans 8:28).

Thirty-One:
HEARING IN THE LAST HOUR

We were called to the Far-Eastern mission field, but we had a big problem - what to do with our house. We could lease it or sell it.

We knew we would be gone for a number of years, and so we wanted to do the Lord's will in this and every matter. I just didn't know what to do, so I decided to spend a weekend away, praying and fasting. I had access to a cabin retreat, owned by the godparents of our daughter, Amy. It was on a lake, about an hour from our home, so I went down on a Friday afternoon, hoping to hear something by Sunday in time for church.

The cabin was real quiet and distractions were at a minimum. The only real distraction was the beauty of the grounds and the lake. I read some of my Bible, and Christian books, sang some praise songs and enjoyed the solitude. On the second day I really wanted to hear from God about the house. By "trying to hear," I was really blocking my hearing from God. Our natural ear is one thing, but our spiritual ears are something else.

Knowing I had to hear in my spirit, by the Holy Spirit speaking to my mind, I was centering my energies on my mind, and not allowing my spirit man to be quiet and hear. I did settle down late Saturday, was relaxed, and ready to hear what the Lord would say about the house, not just what I wanted to hear. Yet, I heard nothing.

On Sunday morning, as I was preparing to go home, I was walking in the small living room of the cabin, when I heard the Lord's clear voice, "Sell the house." It was so peaceful and gentle.

I drove the hour back to my hometown in time for the Sunday service. I was about thirty minutes early, and did something when I got to the church building I had never done - I went through the front door. I had always gone through the side door because that's where the parking lot was located.

As I came walking down the center aisle, guess who met me half way?

The husband of the woman who knew our house was to be theirs!

He asked me point blank, "Is your house still for sale?" I said, "Yes," and he said we needed to talk about his buying our house. God had dealt with him over the weekend, and changed his mind about buying our house instead of being satisfied with his small house. He and his wife did end up buying our house.

When all the mortgage figures were worked out, they paid just a little more for a house that was twice the size of their smaller one. They needed it, because they were to have several more children and definitely needed the room. By the way, when we came back from the mission field, years later, the Lord blessed us with an even larger house and more land.

"My sheep Hear My Voice" (John 10:27).

Thirty-Two:
HER HEAD WIGGLED

Mary Lou, my older sister, was a sweet girl with a sweet spirit. She and her husband, Frank, had three little girls, who were born in California. I received a call from my mother, one day, and she said our sister was diagnosed with great migraines and head tumors. I was astonished, as none of us in the family had suffered from any such serious disease or conditions until Mary Lou had been operated on, several years before, for a growth on her back. This seemed to be a worse condition.

So, we started praying. My sick sister now lived in Atlanta, my parents living about four hours away in one direction, and I lived six hours away in another direction. As time passed, we were told my sister would need to have an operation to remove the growths. This was determined by the top neurosurgeon in my parents' city where my sister had gone for the diagnosis. At the time of her surgery, all of the family gathered at the hospital, except for the little children. As was to be expected, Frank, her husband, was especially anxious and distraught.

We gathered in the waiting room to see my sister wheeled into surgery.

When gurney came down the hall, my older brother and I, approached the gurney and asked if we could pray for our sister. I remember so clearly my brother and me standing on opposite sides of our sister. My brother laid hands on my sister, on her arm, and simply asked the Lord for a healing. Being only a foot away from Mary Lou's face, I saw her head quiver.

My brother looked and said with a quiet authority, "The Lord just healed Mary Lou."

She was wheeled right on through the surgery doors anyway. We went back to the waiting room and waited.

After several hours of surgery, we got the news that the doctor was coming out of surgery and would meet with us shortly. We looked down a long hallway as the doctor made his way towards us. Most of the way down, he was shaking his head. Being a close personal friend of the family, as well as her doctor, we thought our sister had either passed away or her condition was much worse than we had first thought. His steps then seemed to be an eternity for us, as our hearts raced to hear the news.

Finally, the doctor reached us, and said, "I just don't understand this! We took the pictures of Mary Lou's head, only yesterday, and saw the two dollar-sized tumors. They were definitely there. When we opened up her head, they were gone .I just don't understand it."

At that moment her husband blurted out, "Jesus healed her." He started crying profusely, as did we all. My brother, who knew beforehand what the result would be, also rejoiced.

Frank gave his heart to Jesus at that moment, and immediately called a former boss that he had held a grudge against to ask for forgiveness. What an ending to a very tough situation. My sister, and her husband, would now serve the Lord together. Faith is a fact, and faith is also an act. My brother certainly acted in faith!

> "But without faith it is impossible to please him: for
> he that cometh to God must believe that he is, and
> that he is a rewarder of them that diligently seek him
> " (Hebrews 11:6).

Thirty-Three:
HEALED FROM THE ROOTS

I could take it no more. Better yet, I was tired of releasing it, giving it out. What was the "it" I was talking about? Anger, yes, and at times, violent, uncontrollable anger.

Several times a year something would trigger the anger that began as a child, and I would vent and release this on the nearest person, place or thing. Releasing anger came in the form of breaking and throwing things at other people or things; striking out at people, getting mad in traffic, etc. and etc.

This anger of mine, not only hurt other people and things, but it caused devastating effects inside of me. The anger was almost like an emotional paralysis that deeply affected my spiritual heart and mind. It brought fear, with me speculating on when the anger would rise up again. I was starting to live in a cycle of anger, fear and hate, mainly self-hate. I didn't want this, but I didn't know how to get free.

I had been a born-again Christian for almost twenty years, and yet, I carried and released anger, even though Jesus died to pay for it. I had been to four or five Christian counselors that meant well, and tried to help me, but after receiving their ministry, I fell back into the same pattern of anger, fear, and self-hate. To top it all off, I had ministered the Gospel myself in Africa, Central America, the Far East and on the street corners of the U.S., in jails, prisons and the like.

I wasn't a hypocrite living a lie of my faith; however, I just couldn't get the victory over this anger, even though Jesus had already taken care of the anger at the Cross. What was the key or keys to my getting delivered and keeping this deliverance from anger? I finally did something I had never done. I cried out to God! Yes, from my heart. I cried out to Him. I had gone to men for counseling, but as of yet, had not called out to "The Counselor" (Isaiah 9:6).

As I spent more time with God, I came across Psalm 31 where I saw that David had said, "Lord deliver me speedily."

This was not just a random verse in daily reading, but what the Lord spoke to my mind and heart. I was led to call a good friend of mine - Frank - a godly man, who was in tune with God. He told me he believed God spoke to him and said, "If I were to fast and pray for two weeks, the Lord would set me free."

I immediately took this as the "Word of the Lord" for me, specifically. I put everything else aside - work and family (who stayed at a friend's house). I was into seeking God's help, and relying on Him only.

For that two-week period, I fasted all foods, drank much water; read the Word as never before; I walked and prayed, it seemed like several hundred miles. Hope was definitely rising up in me. I felt no healing or cleansing, yet, but I had an inner strength and hope, knowing I was being obedient to The Lord.

Along with the hope, came faith to attach my hope to (Hebrews 11:1 says, "Now faith is the substance of things hoped for, the evidence of things not seen.")

I began earnestly seeking God on a Friday, and on a Friday, two weeks later, I was eagerly waiting to see what God would do. Before I went to Frank's house, there were two trials I faced that showed me what God was beginning in me.

I had worked on a man's house several weeks before and thought I had done a good job. He called me up and was mad. He wanted me to come over and fix something. I could clearly hear the anger in his tone. Somehow, I didn't fear facing his anger. There was an inner peace in me, which I had never had before.

As I got out of my car, to approach Sam's house, I could see him coming out of his house. When he came down the steps, I could see his angry countenance glaring at me. A friendly "Hello" from me seemed to lessen the fierceness of his anger. He showed me what needed to be fixed. It was a tiny screen latch that needed latching. The tiny latch didn't create the anger. It was something deeper in Sam already working, that caused his anger toward me. I knew this from my own experience.

After fixing the latch, I said "Goodbye," and walked away with joy in my heart because I had not reacted to his anger. A few minutes later, as I headed out to Frank's house for prayer, I pulled up to a stop sign. I was quite surprised by what happened next. Apparently, I had cut-off another driver whom I thought was turning in the opposite direction.

With both of our car windows up, and the air-conditioning going, I could hear the driver cursing me out. I immediately waived a "Sorry" wave and backed up. Again, my response to this anger was one of giving-in to the Spirit, not the flesh. In fifteen minutes, I was arriving at Frank's with an assured hope because of my response to the two incidents.

Frank and I chatted a bit about our families, and then we got down to prayer. Frank, a very godly man, has such a simple, but profound, walk with God. Frank asked me to close my eyes and pray.

Within several minutes I saw a vivid picture in my mind. It was when I was a young boy of six, in my living room, celebrating the commitment I had made to Jesus that morning in my church. In celebration, my Dad had a little too much to drink, and he accidentally broke a statue I was given.

In this mental picture, Dad had his elbow on his bended knee. I just knew he was asking for forgiveness.

When I related this to Frank, he said to me, "Forgive him." I did, and at that moment, I started weeping deep down within my stomach. I cried deeply for fifteen to twenty minutes, knowing I was being healed of anger in a powerful way. When I stopped crying, I felt so clean.

Frank asked me to pray again. As I did, I had another mental picture. This time, I saw my mother. She was pregnant. I knew I was in her womb. On her stomach were the two words "hate" and "rejection" and I knew these two forces had entered me as my mother carried me in her stomach.

I also knew she had two healthy children - my older brother and sister - and had had two miscarriages. Even though mother didn't hate me, personally, she hated the fact that she was having another child, and rejected me. I knew, with all my heart, the anger had attached itself to the rejection and hate. Frank asked me to forgive my mother.

I did, and the same weeping, almost uncontrollable crying, started again as I wept for another fifteen to twenty minutes. I felt such a relief deep within me when I stopped crying. I had such a peace, a release and lightness. I knew, as Frank knew, that I was free from the anger. I knew, with all my heart, the rejection and hate which were hidden had produced the anger and was, of course, most observant. This was the key to my healing: anytime I even thought someone disliked me or rejected me, anger would rise up!

Having a praying, godly man lead me by the Holy Spirit, to lay the axe to the root of the anger, I praise my Lord and Savior, Jesus Christ, for my deliverance.

> "And now also the axe is laid unto the root of the trees: therefore every tree which bringeth not forth good fruit is hewn down, and cast into the fire" (Matthew 3:10).

Thirty-Four:
FREEDOM FROM FREEDOM

There were about twelve people gathered that night in our home Bible study in a foreign land. All of them had a sincere faith and open hearts to the Lord. It was such a joy to teach and minister to this weekly group, especially with the excellent interpreter who worked with us. I had known the Lord many years and thus had a number of testimonies to back up the Word of God.

This particular night, I was ministering on the second mission statement of Jesus Christ out of Isaiah 61:1 and Luke 4:18; that is, "He came to heal the broken-hearted and set the captives free."

I told the group when I received Jesus as Lord and Savior that He cleansed me from a very bitter heart for my ex-wife and healed me of an incurable disease - muscular dystrophy.

Later on, I was sharing how I had been to four Christian counselors to get set free from the besetting sin of anger. All of these counselors prayed for me, and were very caring, yet none of them could get to the root cause of my anger, when it still rose up. In utter desperation, I cried out to the Lord and he directed me to a very godly man. Frank was not even in full-time ministry, but I trusted him, and shared from my heart the anger I had from youth.

After two weeks of fasting, prayer and seeking God on my part, Frank led me in a Holy Spirit-directed prayer and I was set free from the roots of my anger - hate and rejection.

As I shared my deliverance, Anna, my interpreter, started crying. I asked her quickly what was happening. Still crying, she said her mother told her, as a child, she didn't want her and how she even went to the hospital to have an abortion. While at the hospital, "something came over her."

She was frightened and ran home. However, all through her life, Anna had heard her mother say how she just didn't want her. At that moment, I asked Anna to forgive her mother. She did.

Then, just as I did many years ago, she began weeping profusely from deep within her belly. The loving group gathered around their sister in Christ and prayed quietly. As I had done, Anna wept deeply for twenty to thirty minutes experiencing a beautiful cleansing from the Holy Spirit.

I was so blessed several days later as I saw Anna hug her mother, and forgive her in person. As they embraced each other, healing and bonding tears came forth from both. Oh, what a profound and precious moment!

Paul, the Apostle, wrote that we are all "living epistles (or letters), read of all men ." (2 Corinthians 3:2). As I shared my deep healing, from years before and Anna heard it, hope and faith sprang up in her heart for the deliverance of the hurt and rejection she had carried deep within her for many years. Yes, Anna received great freedom from hearing how the Lord set me free. It was worth all the pain I went through to see this precious child of God set free.

> " For I will restore health to you and heal you of your wounds" (Jeremiah 30:17).

Thirty-Five:
HE JUST STEPPED AWAY

I had never seen so many pregnant women in my life. Or, at least, they sure looked pregnant. Actually, they weren't, for one of them was my wife, and I knew she wasn't with child. The husbands looked pretty heavy, all of them overweight. So what gave?

They all had many, and, I mean, many Bibles and Bible-related materials up under their clothes. They were in the process of carrying them over the border of another country which prohibited these materials coming into their country.

We were part of a team of fifteen people that day who would take these much needed books into this country which restricted religious freedom. We would take a train, ride up to the border and have to make it through customs with either open searches of your person and/or your bags.

We were led by a very experienced person who might make this trip six or seven times in one day. If you were caught, your Bibles would be placed in a room and you would have to redeem them when you came back through. The officials wanted you to go on into their country, knowing you would spend some money in this cash-strapped nation.

Our group really didn't know each other before we came together for this trip. The group was made up of a pig farmer from Minnesota, a dairy farmer from the same state and a painter from the southern part of the United States - just to name a few.

On the thirty or so miles to the border, we began to talk with each other and came to know one another a little bit better. The incredible thing about this border crossing, was that, at this one place, there were 200,000 people, at least, traveling over the border. During holidays, the border could swell to as many as 400,000!

Of course, there were many different lines you could go through, so our team divided up into smaller groups, separate from each other, so if one was caught they would not suspect the others. When we all moved into different lines, we had our passports ready. We all made it through this part. Then, came the checking of the bags! None of us were necessarily terrified, but as we shared later, our hearts started pounding a little faster.

When my wife and I reached the inspector in our line who was ready to check us out, all of a sudden he just up and walked away. We kept on moving, putting our bags on a scanner, but he was not there to scan anything. As the bags rolled off the scanner, we hurried and picked them up and headed out to the open street to wait for the others.

They all made it out, without a hitch; so much so, that the pig farmer asked when we were going to go through the official checkpoint. He was amazed when we told him we were out! Done!

Caput! It was over. He said, "Really?" We rented a small van to take our supplies to a drop point in the city, left them there, and came on back. I have no doubt that, on this day, we were all covered by the Lord's angels as we went through the border. Praise be to Him!!

> "For You, O LORD, will bless the righteous; With favor You will surround him as with a shield" (Psalm 5:12 NKJV).

Thirty-Six:
IN THE NICK OF TIME

At the beginning of my early teens, in the eighth grade, my life would be changed in the greatest way forever. One day, a neighbor asked my parents if she could take me to church.

During the service, the pastor had an altar call for anyone wanting to receive Jesus Christ as their Lord and Savior. I went down to the altar and prayed a prayer of salvation. I knew that day that Jesus lived in my heart and I would be with Him - forever.

I immediately started praying for all of my family to get saved. When my Father heard about my decision, he was fairly indifferent to my "new found" religion. My Dad had a pretty hard heart towards the Gospel because of a former bad incident at a church.

However, my Mother would pass by my room and see me reading the Bible. This convicted her greatly, and she was saved within a relatively short amount of time.

When I was about thirty-two, married, and with a family of my own, I was invited to go to a revival in a local church. Some of my friends and family went with me and we filled up quite a long row in the church.

About half-way into the service, the evangelist came down the aisle and stopped at our row. He called my Mother out from her seat and prayed for her.

He then told her the Lord was saying to her, "Do not worry, Maxie is going to be okay." He was talking about her hardhearted husband, Maxie.

This man just called my Father by his first name and said the Lord would save him. My Mother broke down and cried. Some in our group were crying and some rejoicing, but all were astounded that the evangelist knew my Dad's name.

I kept praying, fervently, for my Father and I could tell his heart was getting softer toward the Lord. He would even brag some to the guys who hung around his little store that his wife, daughter and son-in-law went to the little country church nearby.

It was in 1991, on a Monday, that Daddy came to me and told me he was going to have a fish fry to start off the revival that week at the little church.

What he told me next thrilled my heart. He said he was going to attend the revival!

He told me I wasn't to tell my Mother about it, as he wanted to surprise her. The revival would start the next night on a Tuesday. On that same Monday night, my parents went to bed, but very early on Tuesday morning, my mother heard a loud noise. My Father was sitting on the side of the bed. He had a heart attack, and fell on the floor.

My mother rushed over to him, and the first thing she asked him was, "Maxie, have you received Jesus Christ in your heart?"

He blurted out, "I just did!" With that he closed his eyes and went on to be with the Lord. For my Father, revival started almost a day early, as he met Jesus face to face. Our God is so faithful!

> "He who calls you is faithful, who also will do it!" (I Thessalonians 5:24)

Thirty-Seven:
KIDNAPPED!

It was a beautiful, sunny Wednesday morning on September 23, 1998, about ten fifteen a.m. I was alone, busily working around the office of the church where I serve as pastor in Jacksonville, Florida.

Our church building is located on a busy street, next door to a prestigious school, across the street from a country club in an affluent section of town. A couple of members had just been in and had left the fellowship hall building when I heard the outside door open, which is usually kept locked.

Upon going out to the corridor to check on the door, I met a young man dressed in jeans and a tee shirt. Rather quietly, he said he needed help and asked for money. I left him in the hall to go to the office to get some of the petty cash that's kept there for such purposes.

As I went to the desk, the young man walked in with a silver gun drawn and said, "I need money, a lot of money."

I nearly passed out, but nervously said, "All I have is a couple of dollars, and you can have that."

He asked, "Do you have valuables like a VCR or cameras?" I then took him to one of our classrooms to show him our old TV and VCR. He didn't want those, but then demanded the keys to my car that was parked outside.

I gave them to him and he said, "Lie down on the floor and don't try anything or I'll shoot you." It wasn't likely that I, a fifty-six-year-old out- of-shape pastor, could do anything to disarm him, but that he could shoot me certainly seemed like a possibility to me.

I remember saying, silently to the Lord, as I prayed calmly, "Lord, I don't mind dying, but I'd rather not go this way."

He tied my hands behind me and tied my feet, ordering me not to move.

He then left, taking my car keys.

After he left the building, I got up quickly, getting my feet loose, and working my hands loose, I went to lock the outside door. Then, I went to the office and called 911. As I spoke to the operator, I heard the man back at the door, so I quickly gave her the information that a robbery was taking place. I hung up and heard a crash, as he broke-in the glass of the outside door and came in. Breaking in the office door, he found me and said he couldn't get the car into gear. He ordered me to get in the car and to drive him. He was bleeding somewhat from the broken glass of the door that gashed him.

I did get in the car and followed his instruction to head north. I wondered, "Should I ram my car into a tree or something?" But then I decided just to pray and follow his orders, not knowing what else to do. He said he needed two hundred dollars to keep his family from getting evicted in Georgia. I'm sure that wasn't true, more likely he probably wanted the money for drugs.

As we drove I asked him, "Do you know Jesus?"

He said, "Yes, I do and if I ever get out of this, I'll never do it again." As we talked, he said, "I don't want to hurt you since you are religious."

That made me feel a little better, although I was still nervous and my chest was hurting me. We drove up to the north side of town to a very quiet residential neighborhood.

My eyes were scanning for a police car, but I didn't see any. I didn't' know whether to slow down and jump out or just keep going. After we had driven around for a few more minutes, we pulled down a lonely street when he told me to slow down.

He said, "Ease out of the driver's seat and get out." As I did, he moved over and drove off. I felt a great relief, of course, although I was still very shaken by the experience. After all, I had lived twenty-two years in the Bronx, New York, in a high crime area, but nothing like this had ever happened to me.

I walked a short way, and saw a man, through the chain link fence in the parking lot of a trucking company. I asked him to call the police. Then I waited the few minutes until a police car came.

After explaining to them what had happened, they told me the officers had found the broken doors and glass at the church with no one there.

Meanwhile, one of our members had heard the news on the police radio and contacted the retired pastor of our congregation who then in turn called my wife, Nadira. She was naturally quite upset, hearing that I had been kidnapped and that there was blood all over the church entrance.

One blessing of this experience was that Nadira was home that day and not at the office, as she normally would have been. The police officers drove me back to the church, where they had cordoned-off the whole area.

Soon, the newscasters arrived and started interviewing me about this big news story of a pastor being kidnapped.

Anyway, that was my fifteen minutes of fame. Nadira and I were interviewed for the evening news and the newspaper. This was not a great reason to be in the newspaper! But anyway, thank God, I was safe, and not injured, other than a few rope burns on my wrists.

Everyone wanted to know if I felt bitterness toward the young man, but I remember praying for the robber, asking the Lord to turn him around. I felt it was not so much him, as the devil trying to remove me, if possible. It sure didn't make much sense to come to a little church, on a Wednesday morning no less, expecting to get a lot of money.

Plus, he had come on a bike from the North side and left the bike and the bag behind! Nadira and I never did feel bitterness or any unforgiveness. In fact, it was very easy to forgive him, as well as feel sorry for him and his wrong choices. It was too bad that he allowed the devil to destroy his life just for the hope of some drugs.

The police officers were very kind and immediately went to work to try to identify him. They took blood samples and finger prints from the church and from my car, which they located abandoned on the north side a few hours later.

What I didn't know, was that the thief was a career criminal and had recently been released after ten years in prison. Two weeks before my kidnapping, he had robbed another church on the north side and hit the elderly secretary over the head with the gun barrel several times.

After he left me, he stopped at a motel and robbed a man from Georgia. He shot him in the arm, when the man resisted turning $5,000 over to him. I was certainly blessed to get off so lightly!

By Friday, a police detective brought us some mug shots, saying they had identified someone from the fingerprints. I immediately identified the robber from the group of photos. The police found him in his mother's house, with a couple of prostitutes, and with several thousand dollars of money in his possession. After his arrest, the two other victims and I identified him. Within months, his trial was held. He was found guilty and sentenced to life in prison for his crimes.

Of all the truths I learned from this experience, the most important was: God has a purpose for me and the devil wants to stop it, if possible. All this has made me more zealous for the Lord and for His purpose for me and our congregation. It was truly a humbling experience to feel so close to death, and to have to depend so completely on the Lord's mercy.

Nadira and I were both somewhat fearful of being alone in the church building after this experience, but the Lord has brought us deliverance from that fear. Of course, in wisdom, we are more cautious now. Some folks still recognize me as the "Kidnapped Pastor," but the bottom line is - we love the Lord, love His people, and want to serve Him until He takes us home. To God Be the Glory!

" Many are the afflictions of the righteous: but the
LORD delivereth him out of them all" (Psalm 34:19).

Thirty-Eight:
MY SON WAS HOOKED

After service, one Wednesday night, a few of us gathered in the pastor's tiny office to pray for some upcoming church activities.

As we held hands, gathered in a circle in prayer, we agreed with one another for particular prayer requests. I felt led to pray for one of the elder's sons. He had three fine young boys who were all Christians. Two of them were actively serving in church as members of the praise band. The older son was also a fine young adult, working very steadily at the local airport fire department. However, he was not active in any church, but still had a heart for God.

As I prayed for the eldest son that night, with the intent that the Lord would draw him to Him, I prayed something I had never prayed for anyone. I said, "Lord, put your hook in him and draw him quickly to you." The very next morning, the older son showed up at his parent's house wearing a ball cap with a big gold hook on the top front! They were amazed, having remembered what was prayed the night before.

Shortly thereafter, the older son was in active fellowship and is to this day. The Lord is so good to give surety to faithful parents who are concerned about their children.

> "And all thy children shall be taught of the LORD; and great shall be the peace of thy children" (Isaiah 54:13).

Thirty-Nine:
NOT CRUSHED IN THE CRASH

I was driving down Ely Road toward Route 4, when I saw lights to the right of me, and I knew I was headed for a crash.

I then looked straight ahead and said, "Jesus, forgive me" because I was in a backslidden condition.

The Lord's peace came over me, and He said, it was "Okay;" He would take care of me.

About that time a strange voice said, "No, duck onto the floor." Disregarding this voice, (John 10:5: " ...a stranger will they not follow, but will flee from him: for they know not the voice of stranger."), I held onto the steering wheel and looked straight ahead.

The next thing I remember, I was sitting in the middle of the road with my legs folded and my hands raised, praising God.

I was unaware, at the time, that I had a broken collarbone. The vehicle that hit me was a propane gas truck. Shortly, I was aware of a mixture of diesel fuel from the truck and gasoline from my car flowing under me.

The truck driver wrapped a blanket around me, and took off expecting an imminent explosion. An old man, who had been sitting on his front porch, and saw the entire thing, came up and sat down with me.

I kept telling him I was sleepy. In a few minutes, an ambulance arrived, but wouldn't come near. They got out a gurney, and told the old man to put me on the board.

Next, the paramedics arrived and took me to a hospital, where I stayed for two days. My car was totally smashed to the ground, with the exception of the driver's door, seat and steering wheel.

It was only a miracle of God that moved me out of my car. I had only a broken collarbone, and lacerations on my arms and legs. I had been backslidden when I asked the Lord to forgive me. He did, and He also delivered me from death. Praise Him!!

"For He shall give His angels charge over you to keep you in all your ways" (Psalm 91:11).

Forty:
NOTHING TOO SMALL

Some call it the honeymoon period. Whatever you call it, the first weeks after getting saved by the Lord Jesus seem like a honeymoon time with the presence of the Lord so close. You have the feeling of "one step closer and you could be in heaven."

After my conversion and miraculous healing in the Virgin Islands, I moved into a missionary house where I did some cooking and cleaning, spending most of my time in God's Word. I also performed volunteer work in the local town. I really didn't have much money, or need for it, because room and board were supplied, along with a very small stipend.

As the days rolled on, I had a need for some ear swabs to clean my itching ears. I just didn't want to poke around in them with any old thing. If I just had one for both ears, that would be a blessing, but I couldn't seem to find any of them in the stores on this island in 1976. I didn't know you could pray about such small things back then, but, oh, the desire sure was there to have them. One bright day as I was walking down the hill out in the country, lo and behold I saw a blue box. I instantly recognized it as an ear swab box. Boy, was I elated. There were three in there, one for each ear and one left over.

They were very secure and clean in the box, so in broad daylight, I went to work on my ears. The scratch met the itch, and with the additional cleaning, I was so relieved. Somehow, I know that the Lord led me right to those swabs. Oh, how He cares for us in the small and little things!

> "But rather seek ye the kingdom of God; and all these
> things shall be added unto you..." (Luke 12:31)

Forty-One:
ONE AMAZING LIFE

There comes a time when you hear a story of a person who has accomplished a task against all odds. Well, when I heard of this one, I said to myself, "There are no odds to this one. It couldn't be done; it wouldn't be done. It was just plain near to impossible to do." But, after really verifying the facts, I found out, it was done!

This is a story of a Miss Higgins from Melbourne, Australia. In 1960, when she was about 18 years old, she contracted a horrible disease, and she had to have her foot amputated to save her life. Next, the other foot was removed. The disease continued to spread and she had to have both of her legs amputated up to the hips. Then, the disease broke out in her hands, and, eventually, she had to have both arms removed. Now all that remained of her was the trunk of her body. As of 1976, she had lived in this condition for fifteen years.

One day, a Pastor went to visit her and was startled to find the walls of her room covered with Bible Scripture texts displaying joy, peace and the power of the Lord. Miss Higgins could still see and as she daily read these Scriptures they burned inside her heart the belief that nothing was impossible with the Almighty God.

She explained to the pastor while lying in the bed that she had asked the Lord what work she could do for him. A short time later, an idea came to her. She called a carpenter friend of hers and asked him to construct a device to fit her shoulder and attach it to an extension holding a fountain pen.

Next, she began writing letters to many people witnessing about the Lord. She had to write entirely by body movement, putting her whole being into it. Nevertheless, her penmanship was beautiful.

All of her letters were written to people who did not know Jesus as their personal Savior. She started receiving letters back from people who had given their lives to Jesus because of the letter they received from her. It has been many years since we've had an update on her, but at that time she had personally received over 1500 replies from individuals who had received the Lord from her witness letters.

Asked how she did this, she replied, Jesus said "He that believeth on me, as the scripture hath said, out of his belly shall flow rivers of living water" (John 7:38) .

The words of Miss Higgins, flowing deep from within, gave living water to thirsty souls and many received eternal life through her. Her natural body was deformed, but her spiritual body was full of life!

> "I can do all things through Christ who strengthens me" (Philippians 4:13).

Forty-Two:
PINPOINT PRAYER

The Church of St. David's Chapel is a quaint little place in the woods about one mile from a tributary of the St. John's River. It seats about one hundred twenty parishioners, at most, with a little standing room in the back. I was a member there in the early 1980's. As a single person then, I so enjoyed the community of believers and the family atmosphere.

Shortly after joining the church, I became involved in an outreach program called "Evangelism Explosion." In this program, we would have preset appointments to go to homes and share our Christian faith using a methodical plan approach. I just loved sharing my faith with others, because I had such a powerful conversion, when Jesus Christ healed me of an incurable disease. We would go out in teams of two each Thursday night. I could hardly wait to go, because, to me, this was just as enjoyable as a good church service.

One night, however, as we gathered for prayer before going out, I really felt led by the Lord to stay in the chapel and pray. This was going against my inward desire because I was so blessed at the anticipation of people receiving Jesus as Lord and Savior. After we prayed, the team leader gave me a prayer sheet so I could pray over a list of the people they were going to visit.

As the team left, I started walking around the small chapel calling out to God in prayer. After a few minutes, something inside made me feel so inadequate as I prayed. All of a sudden, I called out "Holy Spirit, pray through me!" I had never done that before; so it shocked me to say such a thing.

When I spoke this prayer, I started to experience a deeply intense calling sensation from inside of me. Soon, I went back to the spot on the pew and looked at the list of names I was given. It seemed as if my eyes were drawn and fixed on one particular man's name. I knew, by the Holy Spirit, I was to intercede in prayer for this particular person only. I must have prayed a good hour for the person when I heard a car pull up outside and the car door shut.

The chapel door opened and a very excited team member came running down the aisle and grabbed me. I asked her what was going on and she shared with me a remarkable thing. She told me that as they were sharing the plan of salvation with a man in his living room, he didn't seem interested at all. In fact, he had a look on his face of boredom and it appeared he wanted them to hurry up and finish.

However, in the middle of their sharing the Gospel, a startled expression came over the man's face, he dropped to his knees and cried out, "Give me this Jesus you are talking about!"

It was a complete change in his body language and in the countenance on his face. He prayed the prayer of faith to receive Jesus. Then they rejoiced with him and his already believing wife.

I immediately asked her his name and she told me. It was the exact same person I had been praying for over an hour. The Lord sure knows the hearts of people and as we are directed by the Holy Spirit to pray, He does mighty works.

> "Likewise the Spirit also helps in our weaknesses. For we do not know what we should pray for as we ought, but the Spirit Himself makes intercession for us with groanings which cannot be uttered" (Romans 8:26).

Forty-Three:
RE-UNITED BY THE SPIRIT

The reservation lines were long as we inched our way up to the hotel counter that day. There were about eight lines of those checking in for several days of meetings at a Christian convention. Most of the people were older Christians, and, as a whole, there weren't many complaints. They were just patiently scooting their bags along as the lines moved up.

I was right there in one of the long lines, so I just started talking with people and getting to know my brothers and sisters in Christ from almost every state of the Union and many foreign nations.

When I finally received my room assignment, I made my way up to my room. As I entered, I could see several more men had checked into the same room. This arrangement was all settled beforehand, because of the excellent rates we were receiving for us to room together. I unpacked a little and then went downstairs waiting for the evening meal.

Following the meal, we had the opening session. It was about three hours long, but the exhilarating praise music and the quality preaching made the time pass by so quickly. Most of those attending couldn't have cared less about the length of the meetings, because they were truly heaven-sent.

As I made my way back to the room, about 11:00p.m., I felt so blessed that I had come. If I had come just for this one meeting, it was worth it.

As I unlocked my door, I could hear talking inside and I was glad that now I would meet my roommates, finally. Three other brothers were in the room. They greeted me with very pleasant "hellos."

I gazed at one very tall gentleman, and he looked at me, as if we had seen each other someplace. I asked him if he knew me and he said he didn't think so. I asked where he was from and he said the U.S. Virgin Islands. Now, I knew where I had seen him.

"Lucky's Supermarket," I bellowed out! He said, "Yes, that's right."

He had managed the store but was now in full-time ministry. I told him I was saved on the Island about twelve years before. I used to shop all the time in his store. In fact, before I was saved, I prayed for the Lord to come and help me as I was dying, and only had about two years to live. A bag boy in his store had handed me a salvation tract as I went through the line. It became one of many stepping stones to my salvation.

The pastor said he now thought he remembered me. We went over and hugged each other and were able to share many wonderful things that night as brothers in Christ. With about 5,000 attending this convention, it was amazing that I would even see him much less end up in his room. I have since been back to the island and preached in his church. Who can match the goodness of our God!

> "Thou art the God that doest wonders: thou hast declared thy strength among the people" (Psalm 77:14).

Forty-Four:
RUFF CAME OUT OF THE ROUGH

At our home, the night began with an expectancy as to how the Lord would meet us in our weekly Bible study and prayer.

My wife and I hosted this home fellowship group for a few years, on my days off from the fire department. Beforehand, we always prayed for the Lord to have His way.

We also asked Him to bring whoever He wanted to be present, as well as asking that He allow us to personally minister to them by the Holy Spirit.

On this particular evening, as always, we were thankful that the Lord blessed His people by meeting their individual needs. Our hearts were joyful as we said goodbye to our fellow brothers and sisters. One of our close friends, Sam, who was single, usually stayed around a little while after everyone left. He enjoyed our family life, and would, some mornings, even come to our home to pray with us.

However, that night, as we stood on the sidewalk talking, we had a desire to pray for our longtime pet, Ruff, a Benji-type terrier we missed dearly. Two weeks before, he had just disappeared. He was definitely a "dog- gone," forever, we thought.

After searching the neighborhood thoroughly, we had given up hope of him returning. But, that night, we all said a simple prayer for the Lord to return him to us. No sooner had we finished our prayer, than Ruff comes out of nowhere, wagging his tail, as if he had been there all along.

We were ecstatic! We were jumping up and down, praising the Lord right on the sidewalk. What an astounding thing. Where Ruff had been, and where he came from at that moment (it seemed to be from the bushes), just wasn't much of an issue. Ruff was home, in answer to prayer!

"... how much more will your heavenly Father give you good things for those who ask" (Matthew 7:11).

Forty-Five:
SALVATION FROM HEALING

The stomach pains began in 1996, just after Christmas. My wife, Brenda, passed them off as cramps, or perhaps something she ate in the foreign country where we were living. When the abdominal pains increased, she decided to have a sonogram to check things out. Getting a sonogram in this third-world country was not easy, because they are only administered them a few days a week in the hospital. A few days after the sonogram, the doctor diagnosed Brenda with tumors in her ovaries.

We didn't want her to have surgery in this particular country, because the conditions were not antiseptic and there were stories of surgeries being mishandled. Another problem existed. She could not travel to a modern neighboring country for a safe operation, because we had recently foster- cared a little toddler of nineteen months. If Brenda left her for any length of time, the little girl would have emotional damage because of the bonding she and Brenda had already established. She could not take Beth, our little one out of the country until she was officially adopted, which did not occur until seven months later. So my wife, who was in much pain at times, continued to care for Beth and our six-year-old, Angela, while I worked a regular job.

My daughter, a native housekeeper, and I all pitched in to do whatever would help to alleviate Brenda of as much work as possible. The same year, a beautiful young girl from Holland came into our lives. She was studying at the foreign university where I taught. I met her one day on campus and invited her to dinner. We became fast friends with her. Very quickly, she became part of our family. Her mother had died when she was only fourteen years old, and Brenda, became like a mother to her. She would often come over to eat and take hot showers, because showers didn't exist at the university.

Since she was majoring in the native language, she was a great help in shopping and filling out documents for the adoption process, as well as many other activities.

With a month to go in the school term, I received a call, at midnight, from my family in the States to tell me my mother was dying. The call was from my younger sister. She said I needed to come home right away. I told my sister about my wife's condition with the tumors; and, that although she was getting slightly better, I just couldn't leave her. I had such turmoil in my heart over my loved ones in such health conditions.

At about twelve-thirty a.m., I went into our small living room and sat on the couch and began praying. I remember my prayer almost word for word.

I said, "Heavenly Father, you have a track record with us concerning healings."(I was healed of a terminal disease and had known many to have been healed by prayer.) Brenda is your daughter, and I am your son, and I ask you to heal your daughter."

Being very tired, I went back to sleep. At that point, we had prayed for Brenda for five months, believing the Lord for healing, either directly or through the skill of a doctor. The next morning when we woke up, Brenda told me she felt better than she had in months.

She could not get a sonogram that day, so she went with Ingrid the following day to have the sonogram. The same doctor, who tested Brenda before, moved the instrument around Brenda's stomach. He was amazed that the tumors had disappeared.

Although Ingrid was not yet a believer, we had shared our faith with her. She began jumping up and down, saying over and over, "Jesus healed her! Jesus healed her! Just like she said he would, Jesus healed her."

The doctor knew some English, and was smiling as Ingrid jumped around, shouting and rejoicing. Sure enough, Brenda was healed and has had no reoccurring problems.

By the way, I received a call from the States, several days later, and learned my mother was much better. I did not have to go home. She lived for another year. However, this is not the end of the story.

A few days after my wife's healing, Ingrid was on the top her dorm building, sunning herself, when the Lord spoke to her and said, "Why don't you come to me now? What are you waiting for?"

Astonished that the Living God would speak to her, she came over to our apartment right away and prayed the Sinner's Prayer of salvation and was saved. She is now back in her country, serving the Lord. My wife was so rewarded for standing in faith, even as she suffered for the sake of little Beth; and, yet, discovered that God was preparing Ingrid's heart, all this time, to receive the Lord. God used the healing of Brenda to bring about a powerful demonstration of His reality and goodness for others!

> "And a certain woman, which had an issue of blood twelve years, and had suffered many things of many physicians, and had spent all that she had, and was nothing bettered, but rather grew worse; when she had heard of Jesus, came in the press behind, and touched his garment. And straightway the fountain of her blood was dried up; and she felt in her body that she was healed of that plague. And he said unto her, 'Daughter, thy faith hath made thee whole; go in peace, and be whole of thy plague'" (Mark 5:25-35).

Forty-Six:
THE LOVE OF A FATHER

I learned to play the flute in New Orleans, the cradle of Jazz and Dixieland music. Since I was born in Memphis, the home of the Blues, my soul was already primed with melody, harmony and rhythm at an early age. I sure didn't know that my early street music education in these two cities would benefit me years later, half-way round the world - in the Far East.

My wife, daughter, and I had gone there when my daughter was six to do teaching and orphanage work. My wife's and daughter's work mainly consisted of holding babies, comforting and feeding them.

I seemed to want to play with, and make laugh, the four year-olds and up. After three years of age, the chance of one of these little ones being adopted goes down dramatically. So, I was especially moved to bring them some joy in their life. This is where the flute comes in. One day, I decided to take it and play, marching with the kids around the room.

Oh, that day was marvelous. I imagined what the Pied Piper must have felt like as he led the children about.

As we laughed, marched, and danced along around the room in a line, I noticed a little girl about three or four years old standing in a corner. She wasn't being punished but seemed to have found a safe place to be as the others danced. She had a scowl on her face every time we passed. I finally went up to her, and she cringed and the scowl became more intense and more pronounced.

I talked with her, but she didn't respond, except with a greater scowl. As I left the orphanage, I kept thinking of the hurt of little girl in the midst of all the others. I knew most orphans dealt with the pain of rejection. My sorrow for the little one would not last long, however.

About a month later, I heard of a group of Americans coming to China to adopt. My wife was usually asked to come and brief her fellow Americans about transitioning the children from the orphanage to their new parents and life style.

As I accompanied her that night, we were both filled with excitement to meet new parents and children. As I gazed around the room, my eyes and heart zeroed in on the little girl that was in the corner the day of the flute playing and marching. She had been adopted.

My heart leapt. She was being held by her "Dad." I went over to her and introduced myself to him. I then asked her if she could smile for me. She did, as she put her head on her dad's shoulder. He had just had her three days. Nevertheless, the love and acceptance that came from Dad to her had already made a dramatic transformation!

Her rejection had been overcome by love and acceptance. Her father had already and would in the future create many more melodies in the heart of this little one than I ever could with my flute. The Lord had matched up a loving, giving father with a hurting, needy child and the Father's love had quickly won out.

" He sets the solitary in families..." (Psalm 68:6).

Forty-Seven:
THE HOUSE WAS OURS

We had the cutest little red brick house, with a nice back yard, in a good neighborhood, within a short walk to an expansive view of the St. John's River.

My wife and I could have settled down here permanently with three bedrooms, a comfortable den, two baths and a lovely backyard view. Beth, my wife, of a year and a half, had a super eleven-year-old son, Sam, by a previous marriage. I had been in a childless marriage with my former wife.

We both had spouses who left us. We were both crushed, but had both become born-again Christians out of these tragedies. Before we met, each of us had received a lot of healing so we were ready to start anew as Christians in our marriage.

After being married for a year and a half, we discussed having our own child. In March, of our second year, Beth became pregnant. Now, our little house didn't seem large enough after all. We started praying and looking for a new house. Actually, we had only looked at a few houses, when a realtor called us and asked us to look at some houses on Sunday afternoon. We agreed.

After church, we went to get a bite to eat and discussed the houses we were going to see. Before Sunday, we had driven by one of the houses, and really liked it from the outside. As we were eating that Sunday, we were talking about the house we had seen from the outside.

A couple next to us excused themselves and told us they thought we were talking about the house of one of their friends. As it turned out, they were very close friends of the owners. They told us it was a very nice house.

When we arrived at the showing of the house, the realtor was very polite, but told us, since he had talked with us, someone had already placed a contract on the house and he was very doubtful we would get it. Still, we did look through the house. We liked it very much, especially with the spacious back yard, on the adjoining park. The realtor said he would like to show us the other house. My wife said a startling thing. "No thank you sir, this is our house!"

However, the realtor insisted on showing us the other one. Still, my wife said, "Thanks, but no."

You have to know my wife, to know this is very uncharacteristic of her to say this so assuredly. She didn't speak in a haughty way, but with an inner- knowing confidence. I asked her, out of the hearing of the realtor, how she knew. She said the Lord gave her the assurance that it was ours.

Of course, I had to know for myself from the Lord. So that night, I went home and prayed. About three a.m., I woke up with the house on my mind, so I went looking for a Bible in our house.

The Lord speaks a lot to me directly from the Bible, especially about things I am concerned over that are specific and personal. As I read out of different versions of God's Word, I happened to find a New International Version by the couch.

The Lord directed me to Psalm 16. I opened it up and started reading. The first couple of verses didn't speak to me, so I read on. When I got to verse 5 the Lord began speaking to me about the house and property. It reads: "Lord, you have assigned me my portion and my cup; you have made my lot secure (real estate lot); the boundary lines have fallen for me in pleasant places. (Beautiful, enormous oaks bound the house); surely I have a delightful inheritance."

The other versions didn't read quite like this. As I read these verses, I could picture our house and the surrounding property my wife was so sure was already ours. I closed the Bible and went back to sleep, also knowing that the house would be ours.

Sure enough, on Tuesday morning, the realtor called. To his surprise, the other couple could not qualify for the house, so he said it was ours if we wanted it. We did qualify for it; however, we had to sell our house. We put it on the market the next day, and the first person who looked at our little red brick house bought it! In about a month, we moved into our new home, the one with "the boundary lines falling for us in pleasant places." God is good!

"For as many as are led by the Spirit of God, these are sons of God" (Romans 8:14 NKJV).

Forty-Eight:
SOFTBALL IN THE JUNGLE

The year was 1981. I was on the trip of my life - a missions trip to the Philippines. I had already been miraculously led there, but that is another story.

After being in this fascinating country for several weeks, I was having a ball preaching in churches, homes, and barrios (ghetto-like neighborhoods). I had seen many people give their lives to Jesus and saw many miracles by the Lord's hand. Some nights, I only had five to six hours of sleep before my hosts would wake me up to go to another meeting or minister to individuals.

There was never a boring day and the Lord kept me on a non-stop schedule, knowing a rest was scheduled for me when I got back in the States. My third week was to be very different. I was headed to the outback country of Luzon, the northern island of this many-islanded country.

I traveled with my hosting pastor by bus. On top of the bus, were massive numbers of all kinds of luggage and foodstuffs, including fruits, vegetables, and chickens; and, oh yes, people inside! We whirred around mountain sides at some dazzling speeds. Never was I more appreciative of my salvation and assured of where I'd go if we went over the side.

We reached a lovely mountainside jungle compound that night. Actually, it was a combination church, pastor's house and small village. Even though we arrived about dusk, I was greeted by another host pastor, shown my sleeping quarters, and told I would be giving the nightly message in church the next night. Even though there was only one salvation that night, who turned out to be the village troublemaker, my heart was just as thrilled as if many had been saved.

What a way the Lord has. The next day would provide an even greater blessing when we started off through the jungle. We were led by a pastor with a machete to cut our way through some dense bush. It was just gorgeous being out in the northern jungle of the

Philippines.

We climbed a mountain, overlooking the South China Sea, where off in the distance lay South Vietnam. When we were approaching the village, where I was to speak that night, little children would hide behind a tree, because they had never seen a white man.

When we arrived in the main village grounds, about fifty kids were playing softball. I was dead tired from trekking through the jungle, over streams and many hills. These older kids all ran up to me; and through an interpreter, I found out they wanted me to play softball with them.

Even though I was dead-tired, how could I say "No" ?

I did play with them for about thirty minutes and had a ball! I wearily made my way toward a hut, built-up off the ground because of the rains, snakes and rodents lurking around. After a simple village meal of rice and some kind of vegetables, I prepared for the meeting that night. Although it was held in a very primitive building, the love and care of the people far outweighed any physical discomfort.

As the meeting started with heavenly singing, I was caught up in God's presence and a sense of what he wanted to do in this tiny, out-of-the-way village. All of the kids I played with that late afternoon showed up for the meeting. When I gave the altar call, most of them came forward to receive the Lord Jesus Christ. I was told later that playing ball with them had gained their friendship. Looking back, this was the most enjoyable ball game I had ever played and I would do it over a thousand times if the results would be the same - eternal results. Praise be to Him!

> "Suffer the little children to come unto me for of such
> is the kingdom of heaven" (Matthew 19:14).

Forty-Nine:
TRUSTING GOD BRINGS A BLESSING

Mark and Sandi had worked hard that year in their foreign positions. With Mark's very low teacher's salary (Sandi was an orphanage volunteer) and some donations from the United States they were able to make it through satisfactorily, but had hardly any savings.

Their fourteenth wedding anniversary was coming up in April of that year. Mark wanted to do something special for Sandi. He had a one week trip in mind for his precious wife, because they had never taken any such trip in the past. Besides, Sandi had given up her home and much of her furniture to serve the Lord in this third-world country.

For that one week trip, Mark thought of a gorgeous area with beautiful mountains and rivers where they could go. He figured it would cost them about $800.00 for the both of them. This would include airfare, lodging, food and money for a few gifts. He thought, "This seemed like so little to spend for one week," but he also thought about how far this money could spread the Gospel in this country or further their orphanage work. On the other hand, he so wanted to bless his wife, who deserved this and so much more for her daily sacrifice.

Mark finally had a peace about spending the money and went ahead and made the reservations. After doing this, he recalled how the Lord had always blessed them and also had given them the desires of their heart.

Mark and Sandi went on their fourteenth wedding anniversary trip and it was one of the best they had ever celebrated. They rode bikes out into the lush countryside, climbed mountains and took a fascinating boat trip down a fast-flowing river. This trip was a memory that no one could take away from them. It was forever sealed in their hearts, wonderful memories together.

A few weeks after arriving back in their city, they received an e-mail notice that someone they really didn't know had donated to them

$1,000.00! They had never received a donation even approaching this amount. Oh, they were so blessed to know that their loving heavenly Father had touched someone's heart to donate this to them. And they had $200.00 to spare!

> "Delight yourself also in the Lord and He will give
> you the desires of your heart" (Psalm 37:4).

Fifty:
WHOSE REPORT WILL I BELIEVE?

In August, 1996, I did my monthly breast exam. I had only recently started doing this as a result of a television campaign. This campaign is called "Buddy Check 12" and on the twelfth day of each month we are to do a self-breast examination. I was surprised to find a rather large lump.

Due to my daughter's upcoming wedding in October, I decided that I would wait until after her wedding before going to the doctor. I did not want illness to spoil to her special day. Shortly after the wedding, I went to see the doctor.

He told me he suspected it was cancer. He suggested I have immediate surgery. I went in on October 16th. It was necessary to do a mastectomy.

The report from the pathologist was one of doom. It read, "All of the prognostic indicators for overall survival are un favorable."

I felt as if I have been given a death sentence. My oncologists, as well as my four daughters, felt strongly that I should have chemotherapy. I really had mixed feelings about this treatment, but I relented.

One day, during my devotion time, I felt like the Lord spoke to me John 11:4, " This sickness is not unto death, but for the glory of God."

At this point I had to make a decision, whose report would I believe? As I began the chemo, I based my faith on Mark 16:18, "... if they drink any deadly poison, it shall not hurt them."

I truly felt chemo was a poison. Many people were praying for me. There were literally people across the United States and even in Brazil and China praying for me.

Their numbers humbled me. For years I had interceded for China. Now, they were interceding for me. God, my Father, was so faithful. There was no pain after surgery and no nausea during chemo.

I did not always feel my best, but He took me through. When

my blood count would go down, the prayers went up, and so did the count. I knew it was God! Right afterwards, the nurses were surprised I was able to take care of my home, do some gardening and with my husband's encouragement, I took walks. I was then seventy-one years old and felt blessed to be alive. I give all of the thanks and praise to the Lord! It has been nine years now. I am a " Survivor" because of His amazing grace

> "It is the spirit who gives life; the flesh profits nothing. The words that I speak to you are spirit and they are life" (John 6:63 NKJV).

Fifty-One:
WHAT HE PROMISES, HE DELIVERS: The Miracle Baby

My wife, Beth, and little daughter, Angela, were only several weeks into our mission work when we were blessed to visit the local orphanage in this far-off country.

We didn't think we could get in so soon because, as a general rule, foreigners are forbidden to visit orphanages. Even foreigners who were adopting met with officials in a different location to receive their little ones. My wife, however, offered to volunteer and help out in any way possible. We, as a family, were allowed to freely come in and work, as well as get local businesses to donate time, funds and assistance.

The first day my wife visited she was taken into a room full of crib babies. She picked up a beautiful ten-month old girl, which she cradled and rocked back and forth. There was something special about this first one Beth held. As she kept returning to the orphanage, she was constantly drawn to Xing Li. My wife being a woman of deep prayer sensed the Lord urging us to look into adopting this little one. We had never before given this a thought, but I knew when my wife was receiving a Word from the Lord.

We both started praying about adopting and we felt a peace about it. We returned to the States to start the official adoption process. When we returned she asked the orphanage director about adopting Xing Li. Beth was shocked when the director told her that the baby had already been adopted and they were just waiting for the adoptive parents to arrive that week. Papers were signed, money paid and passport for Xing Li processed. It was a done deal. Not according to Beth and the God we serve. Beth just knew she was to be ours.

We got members in our home country to join us in prayer. Well, when it came time for Xing Li to be adopted that next week, the mother-to-be thought eighteen-month old Xing Li was too old and she wanted a crib baby. Being a worker in the UN from the United States, she had clout and the officials overturned established policy to allow her to have another baby. This was the first miracle ! We all rejoiced, then we took immediate steps to foster care Xing Li. This was an easy process for us.

Nine months later, we were told we could not adopt her because we already had a healthy child in Angela. Three days after bringing Xing Li home from the orphanage, we began to foster-care her, a national decree was issued in this country that no foreigner could foster care, nor visit any orphanage, due to another country's exposition of some pitiful conditions in their orphanages. We had just made it! This was the second miracle!

We had Xing Li from the fall of 1995, all through the following spring of 1996. "Our" little girl started calling us "Dadee" and "Momee" as she grew that year. We were so delighted to have her. For five months my wife developed tumors in her ovaries, and wouldn't leave to go to a nearby country to have better treatment. It was nearing the time for us to go home and so our prayers picked up in intensity for little Xing Li. I planned to take my daughter, Angela, back to the States with me at the scheduled time, but was Beth staying, never giving up hope that Xing Li would be ours.

After we were home about four weeks, in the States, I called my wife overseas. When she picked up the phone, I could hear a very loud wind sound in the background. She was in the middle of a typhoon! I prayed over the phone and she seemed to have peace. Nothing had been resolved regarding Xing Li.

One Sunday night, after church, as I pulled into our temporary quarters, I had a deep longing to be with Beth, almost like an aching inside. When I opened the front door, at about 10 p.m., the phone rang. I picked it up and the very first thing I heard was, "She's ours! She's ours!" Somehow the local orphanage went to bat for us. We don't know what they said or wrote to the national government, which has the final say in all adoptions. All we knew was that we were approved to adopt. The third miracle! Xing Li is now eleven years old.

Her American name is Priscilla, which, by the way, means "one of eternal value."

> "When my father and mother forsake me, then the
> Lord will take care of me." (Psalm 27:10).

Fifty-Two:
WITH HER HANDS LIFTED UP

She was a wonderful grandmother, my mother's mother. She came from the country, and spent all of her life on a farm of some type.

Since I was from the city, I used to love to go to visit my grandparents for long periods of time on their eight hundred-acre dairy farm outside our city. My earliest memories of the farm were when I was about four years old.

I had my own pony, and played all over the hills, green meadows and in the ponds. I would watch Granddaddy milk cows, by hand, and, at that age, sure didn't know the reality of such hard work seven days a week.

These were pretty simple days, out there on the farm in the early 1950's. People just went about working the land, faithful, steady, go-to-church kind of folks. On Sundays I remember my parents taking me to my denominational church for a quick one-hour service; and then I would hurriedly walk up to my grandparents' church for the exciting teaching and beautiful singing.

My fondest memory of Grandmother, or "Mimi," as we affectionately called her, was hearing her sing these same beautiful church hymns in their little farm house. But this was not the last memory I had of Mimi. There was one that would have a lasting impact on my life, even years later.

The good times on the big farm were not to last, because when I turned twelve, Mimi got a thing called cancer in the stomach. I really didn't know what this meant, but I knew by the way my mother talked, it was bad.

After about six months of suffering, our beloved Mimi went on to heaven. I knew in my heart that Mimi was truly in Heaven. There was this memory I would hold in my heart, and still do.

A memory conveyed to me by my aunt, something I didn't really see myself. My aunt, who was with my grandmother the moment she died, said she lifted her hands to heaven, as if someone was coming to get her.

As she lifted her hands, a beautiful smile came on her face, she then closed her eyes and "went to sleep." She died, the same way she lived her life, lifted up to the Lord.

That graphic memory would stay right with me through to the time when I lifted my own heart up to The Lord. Even in death, our lives can make an eternal difference with people!

> "Let us lift up our hearts and hands to God in heaven"
> (Lamentations 3:41).

Fifty-Three:
A LETTER A BLOCK AWAY

About fifteen years ago, I read in II Corinthians 3:3 where Christians are "living letters, read by all men."

Our lives, themselves, are the testimonies of the living God, demonstrating how He is transforming our lives into the likeness of Christ.

As I prayed, I felt the Lord wanted me write out my testimony, telling how my life was before I came to Him; and, then, how I came to know Him, followed by a statement about the joy I've found in living for Him. It was to be written in a format that would allow it to be read in about a minute, and printed on light card stock. The Lord wanted me to hand these out or place them where they would be picked up and read. Since I was trained in evangelism, I knew this would be a great way to reach out to many people.

Of course, the testimony would include these powerful things: One, the Gospel of the Lord Jesus, the greatest truth ever revealed to man. Two, the story of the life this great truth had touched and transformed. This one-two punch approach to the Gospel could not miss touching a person's heart.

So I made up several hundreds of these testimony cards, placing four of them on an 81/2 by 11 sheet, and then started handing them out. This means of witnessing could be done so easily by anyone who did not have the boldness to witness verbally. Even my four-year-old daughter helped me hand these out!

I remember one day, while working in a certain neighborhood, I had placed only one sheet out, in a telephone booth. I know, beyond a doubt, that this was the only one I placed out for that day.

A few days later, on Christmas Eve, I received a call from a twenty- something year old young man who said he had picked up the card with my "story" on it. He had picked up the "living letter" a block away from the telephone booth where I had put it. I believe the wind blew it out and carried it down the street or perhaps, someone read it, threw it down and this young man picked it up, read it and gave me a call.

Anyhow, I answered the phone and I heard a hopeful voice say, "Hey man, I need this Jesus." Oh, was I thrilled! The young man was saved on Christmas Eve and was baptized during Easter week! All Praise be to God!

> "For we cannot but speak the things we have seen and heard" (Acts 4:20).

Fifty-Four:
A PUPPY AND A PRAYER

We were always fascinated with back-alley places in the oriental country where we lived and worked. I am not talking about dangerous places you wouldn't want to get caught in, living or dead, at night. These were sort of out-of-the-way places that sold everything imaginable.

You could easily write many books about the sights, the sounds and smells, and the people in the course of their everyday life. One day, as we ambled down one of the streets, there were some people selling some adorable puppies out of a box. These were of mixed breeds and I mean mixed!

The back-alley merchants held out the puppies for us to hold because they knew if we would just hold one of them we would be "sold." Sure enough, we bought one for about $15.00, not thinking of the physical condition of the puppy, or how to get it treated if it got sick. We were just too drawn to the cuteness of the little thing, and thinking how our little girls would be blessed having it.

Our two girls were so happy when we got the puppy home. They just hugged it and played with it and we all became so attached after a few minutes. In a day or so, the puppy became almost lifeless and would not eat much.

We asked around for some help, but there was not much to be given. We did email a good friend of ours, back in the States, who was a veterinarian. He called us and shipped some medicine and other things over to us right away. I had to go down to a neighboring country for some business and so I left my wife and children with this precious little puppy to nurse and bring back to good health.

They did the best they could, but the little guy didn't make it. My wife and children were heartbroken. I arrived back the day it died. My older daughter and I, buried it in a pretty little place that we knew wouldn't be disturbed.

My darling wife, who is so sensitive to things of this nature, took this especially hard. Having a great heart for God and a wonderful relationship with Him, she called out to Him. "Lord, this has been an especially rough two weeks, trying to keep the puppy alive. Please make up for this loss and send us a soul that wants to get saved."

Wow, what a request! My wife wanted the pain and disappointment of losing the puppy to be made up by the joy of leading someone to salvation.

A few hours later, yes, a few hours later, a girl I had ministered to over a two year period called in a desperate condition. She was not a yet Christian, but she needed help from us. Her parents were divorcing and she felt her world falling apart.

She was really considering suicide. I knew the temperament of Sally. She was of the type that could do this. I was not there at the time Sally came over. My wife was able to share with her the good news of salvation through Jesus Christ and the peace only he can give. Sally listened intently and sincerely prayed a prayer of salvation. She was saved, her whole life turned around, and she did have the Lord's peace even during the finalization of her parent's divorce. She received SUPERNATURAL peace that the world could not give her.

My wife experienced the great joy of Sally's salvation and the hurt of the puppy's death was wiped out by this joy. Oh, how the Lord makes up for the disappointments in this life. From this DIS-appointment, the Lord had an appointment with the Holy Spirit and Sally!

> "The Spirit of the Lord is upon Me, because He has anointed Me to preach the gospel to the poor; He has sent Me to heal the brokenhearted" (Luke 4:18).

Fifty-Five:
A WORD AND A SONG

There they were, the faithful eight. These "ever-eight" Christians would show up every Tuesday morning for two hours of prayer. They had been meeting for several years, with the exception of a few irregular participants, the same ones had held up many a petition and praise to the Lord. They had seen Him answer in usual and unusual ways as you will see.

Well, one day I showed up. I was one of the "once-in-a-whiles" who, because of an erratic schedule, came as I could. It sure was a special group to me. Their hearts and voices were reaching the ears and heart of a dear, heavenly Father. Over the years, the Lord has led them to a beautiful blending of song and prayer. These were songs, either led by the pastor's wife or played from a CD player, and interspersed with prayer by the faithful. It was a unique flow.

I showed up on one of the "CD" music days and we started to sing praises along with the familiar, yet heart-felt, lyrics. On this particular day after fifteen minutes of singing, we would stop and pray for about twenty minutes. During the first segment of prayer, a person prayed for her daughter's safe return home.

She had been gone for over a year. Even though she talked with her occasionally by phone, she longed to see her and to have her nineteen-year- old home again.

Immediately, after she prayed, I felt led to go over to her and give her a verse that had popped in my head concerning her daughter. It was from Philippians 1:6: "Being confident of this very thing, that He who has begun a good work in you (her daughter) will complete it until the day of Jesus Christ."

At the very moment I finished giving her this verse, a praise song came on the CD player with the very same words of the Scripture I had just given her! In fact, it was the name and theme of the whole song.

Oh, what faith and love the Lord built in us at that moment.

There are no coincidences with God, only God-incidences. By the way, shortly thereafter, the daughter moved back to her hometown with her family.

> "Being confident of this very thing, that He who has begun a good work in you will complete it until the day of Jesus Christ" (Philippians 1:6).

Fifty-Six:
CREATIVE MIRACLE

We came to know Jenny in the fall of 1995. She was the live-in housekeeper of our Christian friend's parents. Shortly after we met her that day, she opened up what I thought was a closet door at the house she was working in.

She entered the "closet" and didn't come out. I was taken aback when I found out that the "closet" was actually where she slept and kept her belongings. Her "bedroom" was about the size of an American bedroom closet!

There was always a big smile on her face demonstrating the wondrous joy she had in her heart for her newfound Savior, Jesus Christ. You could always spot Jenny your very first step inside a church service, because she would be almost flailing her arms in praise to her Savior.

In our last year of work in this foreign country, we received a great surprise when Jenny came to work for us as our house helper. She was such a delight to have around. She would go about her work singing or humming a hymn or spiritual song all day. At the end of the year, when we were ready to return home, Jenny told us that the doctors had diagnosed her with cancer in her neck. We were heartsick, because we had to return home soon. However, we were able to visit Jenny one last time in the hospital. Her cheerful heart in the midst of such grave circumstances filled our hearts with an even greater love for her.

During the next two years, Jenny was to have six operations. Throughout that time, she led over forty people to the Lord, who were her fellow patients. In addition, three people she prayed for were healed and walked out of the hospital! She did this, even though it was a very uncommon practice in this mostly atheistic country. She was even invited by the hospital officials to come back any time she wanted because they said, "she lifted the spirits of the patients."

During the last operation, the doctors removed half of one lung because the cancer had spread into this area. All the while, Jenny kept up her resiliency by keeping a praise song in her heart. Six months after her last operation, she had to go back for a full examination.

When the X-rays were taken and processed, the doctors found out that the lung they had half-removed had astoundingly completely grown back! Nothing was too big for the God Jenny served and praised daily. Oh yes, she has the x-ray of her lung that grew back to prove this report. Her faith and love for God also grew as a result of this healing miracle. So did the faith of many others.

> "But these are written, that ye might believe that
> Jesus is the Christ, the Son of God; and that believing
> you may have life in His name" (John 20:31 NKJV).

Fifty-Seven:
FROM SADNESS TO GLADNESS

I felt so good about myself that day as I left work in 1983. I had made it through the whole day without crying. I had been rejected by my husband, and then two more men, within three years and my self-esteem was lower than a worm's!

My situation was so bad that I had started living in a state of severe manic depression. Still I had to continue to work because I was a single mother. My boss had compassion on me and gave me a solitary office to work in. If one of my coworkers walked by and casually asked in greeting, "How are you doing?" I would dissolve into a flood of tears. Afterwards, it took a long time for me to regain my composure and return to being a functional, productive employee.

On this day, I drove about three blocks, after leaving work, and then dissolved into my familiar pattern of uncontrollable weeping. I was so frustrated, and wanted to stop crying, but just couldn't seem to get control of myself. When I entered my front door my ten-year old son was there to greet me with some exciting news and a huge smile on his face. I was so distraught that I pushed him away and ran into my bedroom. In a space, about two feet wide, between the wall and the dresser, I scrunched down and sobbed even more.

I cried out to God, not only because of the state that I was in, but also because of the hurt and confusion I was causing my precious son. I asked God to help me and quickly!

I got up from the fetal position I was in, and went into the living room where my son was sitting. I grabbed him, held him and told him I was sorry and that I needed a friend. He softly said with such love and sincerity, "I'll be your friend." I asked him to pray for me, and the words from his sweet and tender spirit were so powerful that I felt a calm descend on me. He then told me that he had had a vision as he prayed for me. He saw me in a pit encased in blackness to my chest. He said as he prayed and he saw the darkness dispelled and light surrounded me.

Right then, the telephone rang and I answered it. It was my friend who had been diligently praying for me. She said she had had a dream the nightbefore and was so excited that I was home so she could share it with me. She said, in the dream, the Lord told her I had a spirit of manic depression and she was to cast it out!

I was astounded! She assured me that there was no distance in the spirit realm and she could take authority over the spirit even as we spoke on the phone. Every time she said the word "manic depression," I got a sensation in my ears like one does sometimes when they are on an elevator and you get that funny feeling.

She repeatedly said that phrase until I no longer had the sensation every time she spoke it. She said I would feel tired and told me to take a rest. I immediately fell asleep and slept the whole afternoon and night.

To this day, I can't tell you what my son ate for dinner that night! All I know is that when I woke up the next morning, all symptoms were gone. I had joy in my heart and was able to face people again. My son and I had great times after that. I love him so much for being obedient to the Lord, for praying his heart-felt prayer, and through his vision, giving me the faith and expectancy to receive what my friend had to share. I have never again heard of someone going through deliverance over the telephone, but God is an awesome God!

> "[The Father] has delivered and drawn us to Himself
> out of the control and the dominion of darkness and
> has transferred us into the kingdom of the Son of His
> love" (Colossians 1:13 AMP).

Fifty-Eight:
FROM BIBLE BASHER TO BIBLE BELIEVER

She was a raven-haired beauty of a girl, who was brought up in the United States North. She moved to Atlanta at an early age, and grew up a product of the late sixties drug-rebellion society.

Although from a middle-class family, she hung out on the streets of "Hotlanta," as it was called, looking for something to happen. She took and dealt drugs, thereby entering a subculture of free love, it's-my-life- I'll-do- what-I-want-to-do world. Belle was opposed to any kind of restrictions on her life.

She viewed the traditional family, get a career, and live in the suburbs life as repulsive. Her tomorrow was to "score" another hit of exotic drugs and pass it on in a carefree life that she and others had created in their own minds. Anything that threatened her fantasy life or made her face up to real life was shunned in dramatic fashion.

One day, as Belle was hanging out around the famous Fox Theatre in downtown Atlanta, some Christians came along witnessing with their Bibles in-hand. They saw Belle, and began to approach her and her friends to share the Gospel.

Before they could begin sharing, Belle grabbed one of their Bibles and started tearing it up. Her wild eyes portrayed a hatred for what she thought they stood for. The restrictions and constrictions of a religion or religious system were not for her. Nothing and nobody would tie her down to a life of dull, daylong conformity to a society she so opposed.

However, one day, a guy came along with no Bible in hand, but with papers he was passing out. He was a sincere and gentle kind of guy, and Belle was interested in what he was passing out. She took a paper. On it was a picture of a long-haired, bearded version of the guy in front of her. As she read the paper, it told of how he had been heavily into the drug culture, just a living for-today kind of guy. It told of how he tired of this life and wanted to know the true meaning of life.

Some people shared with him about Jesus Christ - His life, death, and resurrection for all mankind. There was a breaking in Belle's heart and she wanted what this guy had. The love of a real God, a love she craved for all her life. A paper with a true story of a guy who was standing in front of her changed her life.

She gave her life to Christ and embraced the Bible as His Word, His Way, His Truth, and His Life. Several years later, Belle entered into full-time ministry. No more hanging out on the streets, because One had hung on the Cross for her!

> "Therefore if anyone is in Christ, he is a new creation, old things have passed away, behold all things have become new" (2 Corinthians 5:17).

Fifty-Nine:
FREED AFTER SIXTY YEARS

Many came for prayer to the altar that night. Some came for healing of their bodies. Others came for broken hearts, or wayward children. Some came for a touch from God, and for so many other reasons. My wife, Cindy, and I, had just finished sharing about our mission work in the Far East.

Having shared that night how the Lord had healed me of an incurable disease and an equally incurable bitter heart, many came for their needs to be met by a God who is no respecter of persons.

It was a great blessing to see so many wonderfully touched by the Lord. We had planned to stay in San Antonio for a few days visiting our son, who worked in that city. However, after the service, the Assistant Pastor of the church asked us if we would come into his office the next morning, giving counsel and prayer with someone. We told him we would be glad to come.

Arriving about ten a.m., the pastor introduced us to an attractive, older woman of about sixty-five years old. Later, she told us she was sixty six. We began with prayer, asking the Lord to be with us and to meet this precious woman at her point of need. She told us, since she was a child she had carried around in her heart much hurt and a strong feeling of worthlessness.

We, as Christian ministers, couldn't begin to know the intricacies of her heart, nor just where her hurt began. But, we know the One who knows - God Almighty. We went back to prayer and simply asked the Lord to reveal what was there and what He wanted us to do.

After a few moments of prayer, we sensed the Lord was showing our dear sister-in- Christ the answers, so we asked her to tell us what she was receiving. She said she had a picture, in her head, of herself walking into a dance studio where her instructor was pointing her finger at her and yelling something like, "You'll never be any good." This definitely brought back painful memories for her and she began to deeply cry.

When she settled down, I asked her to forgive the instructor. She did so from her heart and then began crying tears of healing. When she raised her head, we could visibly see she was healed of a wounded heart which she had carried for sixty years!

Our God is great and greatly to be praised! (Psalm 48:1) Although a pointed finger from an angry human being had inflicted a deep wound on a little child, the all-loving hand of a mighty God extended complete healing to this faithful servant of His.

> "... He has sent me to heal the brokenhearted" (Isaiah 60:1)

Sixty:
FROSTY'S HEALING

It was a nice spring day in Jacksonville, Florida. I was taking my boss to meet some golfers who were playing in the pro-amateur part of the upcoming national tournament in our city.

Our printing company was providing a lot of the advertising for this annual event. There was a great sense of expectancy as this tournament drew near. When we met the golfers at the country club of the tournament site, I suggested we all go out to a popular beaches restaurant for lunch. When we sat down to order our lunch from the menu, I sure didn't order what took place next.

Suddenly, I heard a rattling sound above me. Then, I felt a heavy blow to my head and left arm, breaking my chair and the table where we were seated. The air-conditioner filtering system had vibrated off the wall - all fifty pounds of it - and made its mark right on top of me! I was immediately rushed to the hospital in severe pain, with my eyes almost totally swollen shut. Incredibly, the x-rays came back negative, showing no fractures.

For the next six months, I required weekly physical therapy. I was in constant pain in my neck, arm and back, and I couldn't raise my left arm above my waist. In my condition, I just couldn't go back to work. Three weeks later, because I could not physically return to work, my boss, who had helped lift the system off of me, fired me! Through all the physical and mental stress, it was my Christian faith that sustained and upheld me.

After three years of this tormenting condition, wearing a back and a neck brace, the doctor said I could return to work, but only part-time. Since I couldn't turn my head, because the muscles were damaged in my neck from being torn and ruptured, my wife (who couldn't drive) had to come with me to work each day to direct me through the traffic.

It was now going on five years of enduring severe pain and wearing a back brace. My wife, Jean Ann, had to have dental surgery, removing all of her teeth. My pastor and two evangelists came to the hospital to pray for my wife. While she was in surgery, the men-of-God laid their hands on me and prayed, in the Name of Jesus, for my healing (see Heb 6:2; James 5:14).

When they prayed, all of the pain in my neck, back and arm vanished. I had no pain whatsoever! I went home and immediately took off my braces and the electric impulse unit I use to wear for pain relief. I could now turn my head and raise my arm normally. I could even stoop and touch my toes. Miraculously, Jean Anne never experienced any pain from her surgery either. It has now been twenty-eight years since I was healed. I praise God, my heavenly Father, for showing me His great love.

> "And these signs shall follow them that believe; In my name shall they cast out devils; they shall speak with new tongues; They shall take up serpents; and if they drink any deadly thing, it shall not hurt them; they shall lay hands on the sick, and they shall recover" (Mark 16:17-18 KJV).

Sixty-One:
IT WAS FREEZING COLD, AND I COULDN'T OPEN MY MOUTH

I had one of the nicest one-room apartments a single guy could have in a lovely old neighborhood. It was an over-the-garage place with a view of the beautiful St. Johns River in Jacksonville, Florida.

It had continuous adjoining windows around two sides of the apartment. This made the scenic river an ever-present view, with its pleasure boats coursing along. I rented from an elderly lady who lived in the "great house" in front of me. She was a sweetheart and I kind of looked after her daily, checking to see if I could help her in any way.

An incident happened one night that I will never forget. It was in the middle of summer, and it was sweltering hot, even with a slight breeze from the river. I had no air-conditioning and my little revolving fan brought no comfort in the smothering Florida heat. On this particular night I went to bed about ten p.m. I was in a deep sleep when suddenly, at about two a.m., I awoke freezing cold, unable to move at all, except to open my eyes. There, at the foot of my bed, was a transparent-like figure that I knew was a demon.

Fear filled the air, as I beheld this faceless, but ghoulish, creature. I had just been learning spiritual warfare at my church. I had learned about my authority over Satan and his legion of demons, but I never thought I would have on-the-job training so soon. I tried to speak, but I could not open my mouth. I was going to rebuke this spirit-being and command it to go, so I would be done with it.

Not being able to open my mouth, I said twice from my spirit man, "Go, in the Name of Jesus!"

Immediately the creature left and the air became hot again. I could get up and move around. Relief and peace came so wonderfully to me. I had just passed a major exam in my life-class of spiritual warfare, and only one answer was needed: the name of Jesus.

> "And these signs shall follow them that believe; In my name shall they cast out devils; they shall speak with new tongues;" (Mark 16:17)

Sixty-Two:
JOCKO'S STORY

Having left British Guiana (now known as Guyana), my native country, I immigrated to the United States with my family. I grew up in a traditional church when I was young, learned right from wrong, and had a surface sense of morality, but I needed someone or something stronger to belong to. I slowly made my way into the drug crowd, where I was accepted, and felt like I was somebody. I became addicted to drugs. Drugs became what I desired all the time. Yet, I sensed there was a "good side" of me there to help me through those years, from my early upbringing.

My sister became a Christian and I could tell a difference in her. I knew my sister and knew she had more than a good moral make-up. There was a light about her that attracted me. She wasn't just a churchgoer, but a real believer in God. Since she knew the lifestyle I was leading, she was gentle as she reached out to me over a several-month period and shared her faith.

I really started seeing what she had. It was so ironic. My sister was depending on God, and she was increasing in the nice things of this life, as much as I was hooked on drugs and losing everything I had. One day, she said to me in a pretty direct but loving way, "You need Christ in your life." These were the right words at the right time! I knew if I became a Christian my sister would be there for me.

Shortly thereafter, I went to her house late one night and slept in her garage. Her car was parked on the outside and when she went to go to work the next morning the thought came to her to look in her garage. She found me. The first thing I said to her was, "I am ready to go, take me where you want." I was giving up my life, and I wanted what she had - Jesus Christ. She took me to the Lighthouse Ministry, a type of Christian half-way house. I started serving the Lord there, attending Bible studies and memorizing Scriptures.

A while later, I fell away from the Lord. I decided I wanted to live my own life, my own way. However, by this time, I had hidden the Word of God in my heart, (Psalm 119:11). I knew who to go to (the Lord) and how to go. About six months later, I fully surrendered to the love and will of the Lord and came back to Him. I remembered His Words from Hebrews 12:5 "I will never leave you nor forsake you."

I knew with assurance that I could come back to Him. I did get baptized, and now, with the Word of God and the help of my Christian brothers in an organization called Teen Challenge, my mind is being totally renewed and my body restored.

"...who are kept by the power of God through faith"
(1 Peter 1:5).

Sixty-Three:
KITCHEN MIRACLE

My wife, Nancy, somehow twisted her back, which resulted in a painful, nagging ache. When she moved a certain way she could hardly stand it. We prayed for healing, but the sore back persisted.

A few days later, she was standing on a small stool in the kitchen reaching up into the cabinets for something. She cried out as she moved her back in that painful area again.

I was standing about ten feet away. Immediately, the Spirit of God rose up in me, and I rushed over to her and said out loud, "In the name of Jesus, be healed."

She shouted out, "The pain is gone, it is gone!" She has never had any more back trouble. The Gift of Faith was given to me that day to believe the Lord for my wife's healing, and sure enough, the Lord healed her. Glory Be to Him!

> "He gave... to another faith (gift)..." (1 Corinthians 12:9b).

Sixty-Four:
THE DIVINE CONNECTION

There were close to six-thousand Christians at this one-week seminar in 1988.

I was really looking forward to going because the minister, whose organization was putting this on, had affected my life in a great way. Reverend Sims had already been in ministry forty years at the time I first met him.

I became involved in his worldwide work for several years. He was a man of great prayer, who presented the Word of God with power and had already trained over one half million native ministers around the world to share their faith. I highly respected him and I knew that I, and all the others, would receive much from him that week.

The meetings were long, yet no one seemed to care, because the Lord Jesus was held up and glorified. The Holy Spirit's presence was powerful and He touched and changed many lives. About two days into the meetings, I decided to stretch my legs and go for a long walk at lunchtime. I ended up at a fast-food place several miles away. While there, I noticed a group of men wearing badges from the meeting.

I went up and introduced myself and found out they were Singaporean Christian brothers. They asked me to have a seat and we fellowshipped for a while, exchanged business cards and went back to the afternoon session.

The very next morning, I bumped into one of the brothers from Singapore and we both thought it such a coincidence to be able to see each other again with so many attendees. We both promised that if we were in each other's respective countries, we would call one another. Within the next couple of years, I did write one of the Singapore brothers several times and he responded.

Seven years later, after that first conference meeting with them, my wife and I made our way to a Far Eastern country to do some missions and orphanage work. In the middle of our first year, we took a brief vacation to a neighboring country during the scheduled holiday period. We had heard of a good Christian church to attend while there, so we went on Sunday. We stuck around after church to meet new brothers and sisters in Christ. I remember a wide-grinned woman coming up to us and greeting us.

She called for her husband, and two daughters, to come over and meet us. Their name happened to be "Wong," a very common name throughout the Far East.

For the next six years, we enjoyed fellowshipping with them. Kelly Wong had a New Zealand citizenship and would frequently talk about his love of New Zealand, but after several years, he shared with us he was born in Malaysia.

One day Kelly started talking about his brother, David, who lived in Singapore. "Wait a minute," I said, and I described the man named David Wong I had met seven years earlier at the conference. Kelly said, "Yes, that's my brother, you've described him to a tee."

Incredible! This was the same man's brother I had met seven years ago in a group of six-thousand people many miles away! Then, I meet his brother on the other side of the world in a city of six million! They both grew up in New Zealand, but went to different cities to do business.

We have been good friends ever since with the family in the neighboring country, and they have helped us in many ways when we are in their city. Also, we are putting out, by the thousands, the testimony of Mrs. Wong and how she was healed of a brain tumor after she received Christ as her Savior and Lord. Oh, the wonder and majesty of our mighty God.

"The steps of a good man are ordered by the Lord" (Psalm 37:23).

Sixty-Five:
TOUGH STEPS END IN A GREAT REWARD

It was about eighty thirty p.m. when we got the call.

A girl who had just received Jesus wanted to come over immediately and get baptized and in the ocean at that. The sea was right in front of our house, but it just wasn't as easy as going out to the water and baptizing someone.

This particular government, in this third-world country, forbade any foreigner from participating in a religious activity with any of their citizens - in any way! We believed we were living under God's higher law in this respect, and could be active in our religious activities with complete freedom, without jeopardizing the lives of the native people.

We had a big problem though. We had a full moon that night. We would have to wait until the moon waned and the tide went out for the baptism to occur. My heart would not let me get in the way of this precious one, who wanted to fulfill the obedience of the Lord to be water baptized as a sign of true repentance and identification with the death, burial and resurrection of the Lord Jesus Christ. So we waited for the moon's right position and the low tide for about one hour, then we went on out to the beach.

This was not the best night to be baptized in this particular sea. Now, walking through these waters was not like walking through the beautiful waters of say, a Florida coast.

The waters were a dirty brown in the day time, at their best, and all kinds of things had floated up on the beach - dead pigs, trash of all kinds, even a dead body! In addition, bigger fish do come up at night to feed in all waters. I just didn't want us to be "fish food" that evening. I had never released my faith for such a walk in the water, but off we went.

Our first step would require a lot more than faith, as would each step, which deposited our legs up to and over our knees in sand and muck. I don't think anyone has ever given a good description of muck, but just the saying of the word seems sufficient.

Oh, the work it took, not only putting our feet down, but pulling them back out for the next step. We needed to get far out enough out for her to be immersed, so we had a ways to go. I really had not exerted myself this much since the days when I played football and ran track, many years ago in school. And those years were many years behind me!

Finally, we reached a depth that I thought was suitable. I prayed and thanked the Lord for the life of this dear one who had just given her heart to Him. It is such an honor to baptize someone, but this night was so special under the circumstances, and because the girl's heart's desire was for such obedience. After praying initially, I then prayed for her baptism, as I immersed her, saying,

"I baptize you in the Name of the Father, Son and Holy Spirit."

The instant she came up out of the water, I saw her look skyward and focus upward with such an angelic gaze, and I seemed to freeze. She was definitely seeing something. For twenty seconds or so, she held this gaze, and then her eyes and face returned to a normal countenance.

I asked her what she saw and she tenderly said, "I saw Jesus on the Cross!"

No words can describe that moment as we both felt we were in a holy place.

After a minute or so, we trudged back to the beach, not saying a word to one another. The return through the mire was nothing like going out because we were both filled with a holy awe. Any sacrifice for the Lord seems to always bring a reward of some kind. We cannot out- give Him or out-do Him, that's for sure. Blessed be the name of the Lord!

"Blessed are the pure in heart: for they shall see God" (Matthew 5:8).

Sixty-Six:
FROM GENERATION TO GENERATION

When I was growing up, I always wanted a grandfather. My mother's father died prior to my birth, and the last time I saw my father's father was when I was two years old.

I couldn't really say I had a void in my life though, because I had a ninety year old retired minister who lived next door to me, and I spent every chance I got with him. He became my own grandfather, and I followed him around his yard as he did his gardening and yard work. I also lay in the floor coloring pictures for hours as Papa would write or read books in his study. We had wonderful theological discussions from the time I was eight until I was fourteen years old. He imparted a lot into my young life and carried a special place in my heart.

Thirty years later, found me living in China. My husband was an English professor at a university, and I found great delight volunteering my time at a local orphanage, helping to raise funds for special assistance in several areas. Because of my orphanage work, we were considered by some to be missionaries. We found my husband's students quite curious about matters relating to the Bible and we would answer their questions, if they asked.

Professor and orphanage volunteer was our life in China for six years. Our last day in China, Noah, a Chinese friend of ours, came by to tell us farewell. He had just returned from his nearby hometown and said he had brought something to show us. Out of his briefcase he pulled an old newspaper called The Christian Herald. It was dated September 7, 1892!

As he handed it to my husband and me, he showed us the large picture of a man with a huge, long beard. He shared with us that the man was one of the first foreign missionaries in that city and had been a teacher, establishing a school along with starting the first orphanage.

In addition, he had led Noah's great grandfather and great uncle to the Lord. Noah said that during the Cultural Revolution,

Christianity had passed from generation to generation in his family, even though it was so dangerous during this time to be a Christian. It was common for a family member to turn against another family member who was Christian. Not this family though! To this day the entire family remains strong in the Lord Jesus Christ.

As we were enamored with his story I took a closer look at the man's picture and his name. I was curious when I saw the name "Talmage" because that was the same last name of my beloved "Papa."

When I arrived back in the States, I called Papa's daughter and told her about the article in the newspaper and told her the missionary's name was he late Reverend John Van Nest Talmage.

I could feel her smile come through the telephone when she told me that was her great grandfather! It was so amazing! One hundred years later I end up living in the same city in China as the great-grandfather of the man who had imparted so much into my life! By the way, I was the first "missionary" allowed into the local orphanage after the Cultural Revolution.

My husband and I have received so much joy relating this story so many times to others. I am convinced, however, it is nothing compared to the joy the Heavenly Father had when I realized that this missionary was my dear Papa's grandfather. And did you realize the parallel of this story? From generation to generation, Papa's legacy was passed on to me, an adopted granddaughter; AND, from generation to generation, through Rev. John Talmage, Noah's family passed on the blessing of being Christians. Our Heavenly Father is so good and has such a huge plan for each of us, even if it is not revealed for a century!

> "For as the heavens are higher than the earth, so are
> My ways higher than your ways" (Isaiah 55:9).

Sixty-Seven:
NEVER GIVE UP PRAYING

The Eckles were a wonderful family we met during our first year of my work assignment in an overseas country. We did not see Mr. Eckles very much because he ran two restaurants and was very busy, day and night.

Grace, the mother, and Lily, the daughter, became close friends of ours in 1994. Lily was a year older than our daughter, Susan, and they played with each other often.

We had delicious dinners at the husband's restaurants, and from time to time the Eckles would act as tour guides for us around their lovely city. Having no faith to practice, the Eckles' main goal in life was to study and work hard and lead a good clean life.

Being Christian's, and open with our faith, we shared our faith with this fine family at different times. They acknowledged Christianity was good, but there didn't seem to be a heart's desire, at the moment, to receive Christ as Savior. We just kept praying for them and growing in our relationship with them.

About six years later, Mrs. Eckles was selected by her country to go for a summer's study in Israel, outside of Jerusalem. She studied with people from all over the world and met many wonderful people. The students were asked by their hosts not to travel inside the Walled City of Jerusalem as there could be trouble.

One day, however, Mrs. Eckles found out that three ladies were going inside Jerusalem anyway, on their day off. One lady was from Vietnam, another from Thailand and another from South America. They all "just happened "to be born-again Christians! Mrs. Eckles asked if she could go along and they said, "Yes."

Inside Jerusalem, they visited the famous sites - The Dome of the Rock, The Wailing Wall, and the places where Jesus walked, was crucified and was resurrected. Mrs. Eckles bought some pictures and gifts from Jerusalem, which she now keeps in her living room on display.

When she returned home from Israel, I met her, later that year, on a visit back to our city and she related what a marvelous trip she had to Israel, especially to Jerusalem. Next, she spoke to me in almost hushed, holy terms telling me she was not the same person she was before the trip. She was now more at peace with herself and more gentle with people.

She said, "Just walking where Jesus walked seemed to change me." At that time, I didn't feel led to pray with her, but within the year, I had the privilege of praying with her, and her daughter, to receive Christ as Savior and Lord.

After eight years of praying for this family, sharing with them periodically, I was so blessed to see the great work God did in their hearts over time.

> "Then He spoke a parable to them, that men always ought to pray and not lose heart," (Luke 18:1 NKJV)

Sixty-Eight:
HEALED OF CANCER

The bus I was on that day was not so crowded, because it was "snooze" time in this third world country. The streets seemed to be emptied-out at this time of day. I was surprised that the man, who came up to me on the bus, spoke such good English and I told him so.

He said, "Oh not so, not so." He was a manager of a large hotel and he invited me to have lunch with him, I assumed to practice his English. We had a very good lunch and the manager related some problems he was having.

I started to share my faith with him, but he quickly said he was already a Christian, and went to the local church sometimes. I did encourage him to go more often because it would help him with his mental stress and physical problems. I saw the man a few more times and had some pleasant conversations with him, always encouraging him in his faith.

It would be another two years before I saw him again, but under some unusual circumstances. My wife, daughter and I had left this country to live back in America. On my second visit back, there I was walking by the local hospital and I ran into the hotel manager.

He told me quickly that, since the last time I saw him, he had developed cancer, but I was more surprised as he said, "I prayed to God and He healed me."

Running into this man in a city of over a million people was a long shot anyway, but hearing him testify of the healing by God was such a blessing to me. God is so faithful to show us the fruit of our labor in sharing the love and life of God with someone.

To add to this story, on my fourth trip back to this city in the foreign country, I ran into him again in front of a university which was close to where I was staying. He said he didn't usually go there, but he just happened to be close by and we got to see each other again!

"So shall My word be that goes forth from My mouth; It shall not return to Me void, But it shall accomplish what I please, And it shall prosper in the thing for which I sent it." (Isaiah 55:11).

Sixty-Nine:
FROM SUCCESS TO REAL SUCCESS

Sam was a good looking boy, and by far the best English-speaking person in this class, held in the foreign university where I was teaching. I taught in this university in the Foreign Trade Department, one of the top schools in this country. Since I was from America, and the mastery of English has become so critical in world trade, these students hung on to every word I said.

I could see Sam was, at times, very frustrated with the students as they struggled with English. His impatience seemed to stem from pride and a self-sufficient attitude.

Sam and I became good friends that year. I introduced him to some other foreign teachers, whom he liked, and made regular contact with them. After Sam's graduation from the university, his career in foreign trade would follow. He became an apprentice at a local company, where he worked many long hours, and with very low pay. He was given a room and two meals a day.

However, Sam was energetic and enterprising. He knew where he wanted to be five years down the road. After his "probation time" he struck out on his own, moving up fast with a foreign company. He worked for a shoe company from Italy, and traveled there and to the United States. Sometime between his graduation and his early work years, some of the friends I introduced him to led him to salvation in Jesus Christ. He lost a little bit of his pride, but most of his self-sufficiency was still there.

We would fellowship with Sam from time to time, and he would help us out with any practical things in his native country. He did attend Bible studies faithfully, but mixing overseas trade with Christianity was a struggle. He grew restless, and I knew something great was troubling, but he just wouldn't open up. In the midst of his deep struggle, there was an incident that put Sam over the edge and got him in the Lord's corner for good.

While traveling back from a city late one night, he hit three people on the road, injuring them seriously. It wasn't long after the accident, Sam answered God's call on his life to enter full-time ministry.

Since turning his entire life over to the Lord, he has had to rely on the Lord for everything, even where his next meal was coming from. Just talking to him, we can hear the humility in his voice, and true dedication to the Lord and His work. He is now a person whom the Lord can shape for His wonderful purpose and use. Sam could have hardened his heart after the accident, and gone on his own way, as he had so many times before. This time, however, Sam yielded his life to the Prince of Peace, Jesus, and is now getting to know the One who ultimately controls everything, anyway. Sam has found true success!

> " Trust in the Lord with all your heart and lean not to your own understanding" (Proverbs 3:5-6).

Seventy:
GOD SENT YOU, DIDN'T HE?

We had served on the mission field for six years in a certain country.

During that time, we had adopted a precious little girl, who has just turned nine and is thriving in every way. Our work in the orphanage was to assist with the daily care of the orphans, and help up-grade the facilities through donations. Since we left this country and have begun living back in the States, I have traveled back and forth to this foreign land helping with daily supplies and any other assistance we can give. I usually go with a local interpreter to survey the present needs or take something we were donating.

On one particular trip, I had arrived in this foreign city and planned to visit the orphanage in a few days. Arriving at the orphanage, with my interpreter, the director and some of her staff, and I, cordially greeted each other.

Before I could start a conversation, the director blurted out, "God sent you didn't He?"

Well, I was shocked to hear this from her because in her country religious activities are severely restricted, and mentioning God is not a very dominant conversation piece. Usually, I would be careful how I answered for fear I would be baited into saying something that would get me into trouble.

However, since she asked, I said, "Yes, He did."

From this point on, I was able to share my personal testimony and the gospel of the Lord Jesus Christ. The director and her staff listened intently as the Holy Spirit sowed the seed of His eternal salvation. Originally, I was going there to check on the needs of the orphans, but the Lord had other immediate ideas -- to show the director and her staff their eternal need of salvation!

> "How beautiful are the feet of those who preach the gospel of peace. Who bring glad tidings of good things" (Romans 10:15).

Seventy-One:
DEATH COULDN'T HOLD HER

It was about eight p.m. when I arrived home that night. After greeting my precious wife and two daughters with a hug, I sat down to a late dinner. I was physically and mentally tired that night. I just wanted to eat, relax a little and go on to bed.

About ten minutes into the meal, I received a call from a dear Korean woman from our church, pleading with me to come to the Intensive Care Unit of one of the local hospitals. A woman had tried to committed suicide and was on total life support. Sensing the hopelessness of the situation, oh how my body and mind fought my heart with the urge to say "no" and to ask if I could come in the morning. My heart won out and I hurriedly got dressed for a hospital visit and headed on out.

Arriving about 9:30 p.m., I had no trouble getting into the ICU with my minister's credentials. I spoke with the head nurse, who was as kind and helpful as she could be. I hesitated going in to see Clara, and instead started telling the nurse how I had been miraculously healed of Muscular Dystrophy. This happened twenty-seven years ago after I became a born- again Christian.

She was very open to hearing my testimony and the Gospel of Jesus Christ. She thanked me for speaking with her and I went in to see Clara.

It was very quiet at that time in ICU and I just stood at Clara's bedside gazing at all the tubes and machines that were keeping her "alive." A doctor came in, checked the machine readings, and opened one of Clara's eyes. There was nothing but a blank, dead stare - no life at all.

Things just didn't look good, by natural standards, with the comatose state she was in. After everyone left the room, I did something I had never done before when praying over someone. I sang a praise song over her in a very low voice so no one could hear.

After that, I spoke to her in a commanding voice three times,

"Life, life, life." Then I asked the Lord what else I should do, and I heard Him speak to my heart, "Be still and know that I am God. (Psalm 46:10)"

Oh, what a verse for the moment! I have asked the Lord to heal others before and He has done it, but this was so different this time: I spoke life to her!

According to the scriptures, Jesus heard what the Father told Him to do all the time and He did it. I felt so led of the Holy Spirit of God, not to ask the Lord to heal, but spoke right out of my spirit, "Life, Life, Life!" and went home that night with a built-up faith, considering the circumstances.

Two days later, Clara's husband came to the hospital to ask the doctor to take his wife off life support. The doctor checked her before he would pull the plug, and said, "You don't understand; this is remarkable! There is self- sustaining life now in your wife. We can't allow her to die." In three days, Clara was walking around her hospital bed and in a week she was out of the hospital.

Praise to the Lord! He still raises the dead!

> "Jesus Christ the same yesterday, and today, and forever" (Hebrew 13:8).

Seventy-Two:
GRACE FOR GRACE

It was August, 2001, and the school year had started off like any other. My daughter, Grace, was excited to be in the third grade and my son Luke was busy with sixth grade activities. We had no way of knowing how our lives would be irrevocably changed that year!

Grace was out on the playground during recess. She had decided to try to walk across the top of the dome-shaped jungle gym without using any hands to hold on. She had already done it once, successfully, so she was unafraid to try again.

As she got to the apex of the dome, her feet slipped. She fell through the bars, hitting the right side of her hip on the bar, and then landing on that same hip when she hit the ground. She was in terrible pain. This accident started what seemed to be endless visits to Nemours Children's Clinic.

Our doctor initially thought that she had fractured her pelvis. She was in so much pain that he ordered a wheelchair for her to use. Eventually the fracture was ruled out, but the pain persisted. Grace was wheelchair bound for several weeks. Instead of her pain decreasing, it seemed to be getting worse.

She began physical therapy, which proved to be tortuous for her. She cried so loudly that the therapists would have to work with her in a private room.

Very little work was being accomplished because of her pain level. Within a matter of weeks Grace had gone from being an extremely active and spirited child to one who was having tremendous difficulty just making it through a normal school day, even with the assistance of the wheelchair.

During this entire ordeal our family and friends were praying God would heal Grace in whatever way He chose. We kept her in school, piano, and involved in church activities, believing that keeping her life as normal as possible would be the healthiest choice for her.

After several weeks of physical therapy, the doctor decided to admit Grace to the hospital since her pain level had not diminished. Several tests were run, including blood work, MRI, Bone Scan, and an EMG.

Nothing of real importance showed up on the tests, so the team of doctors decided that Grace had incurred nerve damage with a small hematoma located in the hip. They said this type of nerve damage wasn't permanent, but it could take up to six months to completely heal. They also told us the hematoma would be absorbed by the bloodstream and was of no real consequence.

Well, we were thrilled with this report! The only problem was the very real one of Grace's pain. She cried every time she was moved, or even when we went over a small bump in the road! The thought of her being in this amount of pain on a daily basis, especially during therapy, was overwhelming for all of us.

Two weeks after the diagnosis, Grace had progressed to using crutches and was out of the wheelchair. One Saturday evening, when she went to bed, her father had a heart to heart discussion with her. He told her that she needed to stay positive about her recovery and getting well.

She told us later, that when he left the room, she began praying privately for her healing (which she did frequently). She decided that she would pray all night on her own and ask God to heal her.

So off and on throughout that night she would ask God to heal her body. When she woke up on Sunday morning, she told the Lord, "Now God, I don't know if you chose to heal me or not, but I'm going to try to walk!"

My husband had already headed to church and I was busy in my room getting ready. Gracie came in using only one crutch. I was so excited! This was quite an achievement!

Grace was excited, too. Being the mother that I am, I encouraged her, but also warned her to be careful and not to go too fast.

Within just a few more minutes, Grace was running and jumping in the house! My son and I couldn't believe our eyes! She had been completely healed. There was no limp, no pain, nothing!

Complete and utter joy engulfed us as we made one of the sweetest phone calls ever to her father. Imagine the delight and joy of those in our church family as Grace emerged at church that morning walking totally on her own and telling everyone how God had chosen to heal her.

This incident occurred over four years ago. Grace has an unshakable faith in God, the Father, and His Son, our Lord Jesus Christ!

One day not long ago, we were reminiscing about the whole event and I asked her why she thought God chose to heal her in such an incredible way.

She answered, "I don't know Mom, but I've been thinking that if I'm ever a missionary, and I'm telling other people about Jesus, no one can tell me what happened to me didn't happen - I know that it's true!"

Isn't God sweet to reveal Himself to those who put their faith in Him? I have been constantly reminded of the verse in Matthew 19:14:

"Jesus said, 'Let the little children come to me, and do not hinder them, for the kingdom of heaven belongs to such as these.'"

Oh, that we may always approach Him with childlike faith and wonder! I know the plans God has for Grace are wonderful, and I know this part of her testimony will sustain her through whatever lies ahead of her in life.

She will truly be able to say, "O Lord my God, I called to you for help and you healed me!"

> "O, Lord my God, I called to you for help and you healed me" (Psalm 30:2).

Seventy-Three:
I KNOW THEM!

Our little Joy was indeed a bundle of joy, and she was finally ours.

Officially ours! All the papers were signed, the full payment made and we were on our way out of Joy's native home. She was a miracle adoption for us, in view of the fact that someone else had already been assigned Joy and had completed the adoption process, except to sign the official papers and make payment.

When the couple came to pick her up, however, the prospective mother said Joy was too old and she wanted a crib baby. Joy was eighteen months old at that time. Since the woman was a UN official, she apparently used some of her "clout" to challenge the established adoption procedure - something totally unheard of in this particular Asian country.

We had already had her in foster care for eighteen months. So, God gave us the desire of our heart - little Joy. However, I had one obstacle to overcome - how to get over the border, in time, so I could get to the airport to meet my flight.

The only thing for me to do was to call our travel agent and see what she could arrange. I called Alice knowing, with her professional service and that she would work something out. She said the only way I could go was by train across the border. This would be very difficult because I had never before taken the train in this country, and knew just standing in line for a ticket, with the massive numbers of travelers would be an almost impossible feat for me - especially with a baby, suitcases, stroller, and a diaper bag.

While I was talking with Alice, I heard someone else saying something over the phone. A man was making reservations for the exact city I was in. He was only coming for a day. He had overhead Alice say my name and asked if, "Peter was her husband." She said, "Yes." The man said, "I know them! I will arrange my schedule to escort her and her baby back to her destination. I know how to get around on the train."

With his help, I made it in time to catch my flight home. This man, who knew us, "just happened" to be in the travel office at the same time I called from an adjoining country. God is so faithful to meet us at our point of need!

> "And we know that all things work together for good to them that love God, to them who are the called according to his purpose" (Romans 8:28).

Seventy-Four:
I DIDN'T RAISE MY HAND

What a wild ride I was having around mountain curves, skirting the edge of deep-valley crevices. I was on a bus journey up the northwestern coast of Luzon, Philippines, going to visit a pastor I had just met in Manila. He had a countryside church bordering on some of the thickest jungle overlooking the South China Sea.

I had spent some wonderful times with him, and some other Pastors, in a large crusade in Manila. After the crusade, he asked me to come up to his church, stay a few days and minister. Little did I know that these jungles were filled with rebel hideouts and dangerous animals. Well, as they say, what you don't know won't hurt you.

Pastor Emanuel had a small, but active church which bordered on a river, used for washing clothes and bathing. I was given a small room for my accommodations, with a quiet place for reading and praying. I had ministered in many different places in Manila - churches, houses, and street meetings - but this was my first time ministering in a jungle village setting.

When I entered the church that night, I was greeted by a number of young people, so friendly and gracious. Their smiles and joy were instantly infectious and touched my heart deeply. Following some beautiful praise music, I was called upon to speak. My whole message was salvation by faith in Jesus Christ. Even though it's the same message, it is never old, but is as if I had preached it for the first time. Of course, following the message, I gave people a chance to come forward for prayer if they wanted to receive Jesus as Lord and Savior.

At the first call, no one came. And after the second call, no one came! Yet, I knew in my heart that some should come. I just knew. I offered a third call to receive Jesus, and lo and behold, in the very back of the church a hand shot up. At that moment, I did something I had never done - ever - I raced down the center aisle and put my arm around the young fifteen-year- old who raised his hand.

When I commended him for wanting to receive Jesus, he said to me, "But I didn't raise my hand, something raised it for me!"

I asked him if he still wanted Jesus as His Savior and he said, "Yes."

The congregation of about a hundred went wild.

I led him in a sinner's prayer up front and afterwards there was great rejoicing. If I had traveled all that way on a bus with chickens, pigs, people and luggage for this one young man, it was worth it.

Later that night, I found out this young man was the troublemaker of the village. Much prayer had gone up for him. I believe with all my heart, God sent an angel to raise his hand that night, and me, to personally ask the question of salvation to really move his heart.

Oh, what the Lord will do for one soul.

> " Angels rejoice over one soul who repents" (Luke 15:10).

Seventy-Five:
MIRACLE AFTER MIDNIGHT

In October, 2001, I was diagnosed with the deadly melanoma cancer. I had been having a great deal of pain in my neck and shoulder. Even wearing a loose shirt around my neck was difficult.

The doctors cut a large size wedge out of my shoulder in order to remove the damage done by the tumor. Still numerous tests and x-rays showed that the cancer was spreading up my neck.

The doctors gave me no hope. The best they could offer was to try to extend my life a bit and make me comfortable. My mother was sitting next to me when the prognosis was given.

She began to cry and ask God, "Why?" My mother had never been one to pray out loud or really be vocal in her faith. So, I was surprised to hear her pray aloud, asking God to heal me.

My condition deteriorated over the next couple of months. Fear so gripped me that I couldn't eat, sleep or even move about much. I questioned God, asking Him what I had done to deserve this. At this point, my faith was in my works, not in Him.

When God revealed this to me, I fell to my knees and asked the Lord to forgive me for my doubt and unbelief. I surrendered my life to Him and began to study God's Word as my daily food. I knew He had the answers.

Very early one morning, about two a.m., several weeks later, I awoke from a peaceful sleep. The television was on a Christian station.

As my eyes began to focus, I saw a preacher holding his hand up, saying, "There is a brother with cancer in the neck and shoulder area. Your faith has just healed you!" I felt a warm feeling come over me and I fell to my knees crying. I knew that God had just healed me.

A few days later, I was scheduled for surgery to try to remove the mass. I was on the table, going under the anesthesia, confident the Lord had healed me. When I awoke, my surgeon said that it was in a bad place and it was too dangerous to remove. However, what puzzled him was that it did not look like a tumor now. So, he scheduled an additional test.

One week later, the results showed that I was cancer free. The cancerous tumor was now simply a fluid-based cyst. Hallelujah! I have never had anymore pain. This was truly a miraculous intervention! God truly does love us that much! It is my joy to spend the rest of my life telling the world of His unconditional love.

"... But say the word and my servant will be healed"
(Luke 7:7).

Seventy-Six:
PACKAGE DEAL

It was November of 1975, and I felt I was the most alone and desperate man aboard a flight out of New Orleans for the U.S. Virgin Islands. At the time, I thought I would spend the rest of my life there - a life, according to medical doctors, that wouldn't last another four or five years.

You see, I was diagnosed with an incurable muscle-degenerating disease where my muscles would wither away and I would end up in an iron lung gasping for breath. I should have had more than double the life span in front of me, but I was truly facing a sure death sentence in a few years.

I chose the Virgin Islands because they were American, and I could work and live there. Second, I loved to sail and dive, having done both in the beautiful tropical waters of Florida and Jamaica.

Third, I surmised, "If you're going to die in this way, what a way to go."

I definitely knew, at the time, it would be much better in a warm climate than struggling against the cold in some northern area of the States. I arrived in St. Thomas, Virgin Islands with enough money for living expenses for a couple of months, while I looked for work.

This type of disease is a slow, progressive disease of muscle deterioration which made me tire quicker, but I could still work.

After a few weeks, I got a job at a seaplane company, in maintenance, working from six-thirty a.m. to two-thirty p.m. - great hours to hit the beach and partake of all the water sports. I settled in to the much slower paced island life. My whole system seemed to slow down and I could just be still and think about life.

I wasn't a drinker, so I didn't get lost in alcohol due to my circumstances. I could get addicted just by getting a high standing on the fore hull of a Catamaran as I sailed from island to island, inhaling all the sun and wind I could, marveling at the wonders of the blue-green Caribbean beneath me. After these trips, I experienced a peace and calmness that nothing had ever given me.

Yet, I lived with death facing me. At times, there was a foreboding veil that seemed to envelop my mind and heart - a tremendous fear, not knowing what was on the other side of death.

I had been brought up in a church, had heard about heaven and hell, and I knew I wasn't a candidate for the former, but a most likely one for the latter. I hadn't gone to church in years, except for weddings and funerals. I sure wasn't a religious person, never thinking about God, and I sure didn't know how to pray. Somehow, I wasn't mad at God, but thought my present condition was just punishment for basically forgetting God and living such a selfish life.

One night, I rode my motor bike on top of a mountain. I came upon a cemetery, got off my bike and went over and sat on somebody's tombstone. I had not planned this, I just ended up there.

As I gazed out at ten million water-sparkles from a near full moon shining on the sea, I pondered the ever-present deterioration of my mortal body.

As I sat there, I uttered a weak and feeble prayer: "Jesus, God please help me."

I felt nothing, and my thoughts wandered off into the night. However, within two weeks after I said that simple prayer, I met some people at work, who shared the gospel of Jesus with me.

Additionally, at the beach I went to several times a week, a young man came up to me and handed me a piece of paper with the message of Jesus on it. A few days after that, a grocery clerk who frequently checked me out and bagged my food, handed me another Gospel message!

Did someone hear my prayer? Something was happening! In such a short time, after I prayed, all these "meetings" occurred. Even after these "divine connections" there was one that had a lasting impact.

One Saturday, I was playing my flute between two buildings for the acoustical effect. There, a fellow walked up to me and introduced himself. His name was Cyrus. He said that I played a "mean" flute (meaning I was pretty good).

He asked me if I'd like to jam sometime with him as he played his flute and the Conga drums. I said "Sure."

So late one Saturday afternoon, I showed up at Cyrus' home and we jammed for a little over an hour. At the end of the session, he asked me if I'd like to attend a Bible study he was having in his house that night.

At first, I said, "No," but then changed my mind. I was really struck by his sincerity and love. When we went downstairs from the loft, I was startled to see about forty young men and women sitting on the floor waiting for someone to give the study. We started off with singing and finished up with a Bible study of about one hour. I felt a lot of love from the group, as I was encouraged to become a Christian through accepting Jesus as my Lord and Savior.

Shortly thereafter, I picked up a small Bible and started reading it. It was filling my heart with hope as I read where Jesus healed all kinds of diseases, mended broken hearts and gave eternal life to all who received His death on the cross for our sins.

However, in the midst of this very hopeful time, I could feel some evil pulling at me, thoughts that accused God and doubted the Bible. I had never felt such a war going on in my mind and heart. One day, in an act of despair, I threw the Bible away. I was angry with God for not saving me. I thought He was playing games with me. I rode my motorbike down to the beach (my sensual addiction to lessen the pain of the anger and frustration). When I arrived at the beach on a beautiful, gorgeous and sunny day, I immediately saw a tent set up that I had never seen. As I approached the tent, it started to pour down rain without a cloud in the sky. I ran my bike under the tent, where a little island boy, about six years old, came up and said they were having a revival that night and would I come.

Instantly I said in my heart, "God, why don't you leave me alone?"

I couldn't get mad at the precious little boy. It was God speaking through him - "Won't you come, won't you come?"

I said I might, lying all the time.

When the rain stopped, I, in my anger, got on my bike and rode out to the east end of the Island to Cyrus' house and his mission buddies. When I walked up the hill I could see them out on the balcony with their shiny faces; and as I approached, I could tell they noticed my not-so-shiny face, but a face of anger.

When I stepped on the porch, they greeted me with love and acceptance and invited me to have dinner with them. Their love really softened my heart and hope seemed to be rising up in me.

After dinner one of the Christians and I were talking out on the balcony.

He challenged me in a very gentle way with two statements.

He said, "If you ask Jesus to come into your heart, to forgive you of your sins, and He isn't real, you've only lost a little breath. But, if you sincerely ask Him to be Lord and Savior, and He is real, then you have gained the universe."

I will never ever forget those two statements. In a matter of several minutes, I prayed with him to receive Jesus as Lord and Savior. Then, I knew something happened on the inside of me. I spent the night with them, and got up the next morning with a peace I had never had before.

Four days later, I met a missionary who asked me to an inter-denominational meeting. People there were singing, and then giving examples of how God changed and touched their lives.

At the end of the meeting, the leaders came over to me and asked if they could pray for me.

I said, "Of course."

You couldn't visibly tell I was sick, but someone had told them. After they prayed, a few of them drove me home. When I got out of the car and waved goodbye, I walked a few steps and then was enveloped by the most majestic feeling of love I have ever experienced.

I started raising my hands and praising Jesus. Oh, it was such a glorious experience at elevenp.m. at night. I had received what the Bible calls "the power to witness" (Acts 1:8) or the Baptism of the

Holy Spirit.

I couldn't go to sleep that night, until I shared with someone what Jesus had done in my life. Amazingly, taking a flight to an island that I hoped to die on, I found life - eternal life, through Christ. By the way, the muscle spasms, a sure outward sign of the disease, stopped in my body. In three months all my degenerated muscle tissue grew back!!!

> "The Spirit of the Lord GOD is upon me; because the LORD hath anointed me to preach good tidings unto the meek; he hath sent me to bind up the brokenhearted, to proclaim liberty to the captives, and the opening of the prison to them that are bound; To appoint unto them that mourn in Zion, to give unto them beauty for ashes, the oil of joy for mourning, the garment of praise for the spirit of heaviness; that they might be called trees of righteousness, the planting of the LORD, that He might be glorified" (Isaiah 61:1-3).

Seventy-Seven:
WALKING AFTER NINETEEN YEARS

I can see Lance today, as if it happened only yesterday, tapping his fingers on the arms of our rocker in the living room. He was almost desperate - about to give up! About what?

The Lord had brought him to this foreign country to serve Him and win souls, still, after ten years he had only seen a few results. This was our first year in the same country, and we were having some pretty good results. My heart really went out to him, because it was not easy living in this land and you could definitely see the call on Lance's life.

Before Beth and I left to come overseas, we had been in a series of true revivals where the Spirit of God was moving and changing lives. We were greatly touched, and prepared to serve the Lord in this land. We were given some tapes of the meetings, twelve in all, and I felt led to give these to Lance to see if they would stir him up, and give him hope for carrying on in his work.

I gave him three at a time.

Given that he lived just forty-five minutes away from us in a smaller town, Lance would come back to our city all excited when he had listened to the tapes.

He said, "Is this really happening in America?"

We assured him it was. He would take three more, and after really listening to the twelve, he said he had renewed hope now in what God wanted him to do.

In a month or so, he would travel back to his home country of Australia. What he found in his local church was the same movement of God was happening there as well. Well, Lance was ready to receive from the Lord, having been primed by the cassette tapes and our encouragement, the Spirit of the Lord really touched him, and he came back a new man to the country he was called to serve.

He came over for a visit and shared with us how the Lord wanted to use him in a powerful way. He was not cocky, but humbled and resolute, now that he had power, desire and obedience from the Lord to do mighty works. Did he pump us up! We were reaping from sowing into his life and we were being stirred up that much more. It was not long after Lance's return visit that he came to see us with an incredible story.

He reminded us we had given him a video tape of an evangelist whom God had blessed with the gifts of healing. This evangelist always admitted he had no power in and of himself, but it was the Lord who did all the work. My wife was healed by the Lord of scoliosis of the spine in one of his meetings. Lance kept looking at the video tape, and the working of God embedded it deep within his spirit. He had an added faith, and boldness, to do the same works Jesus did when He was on the earth.

In prayer one day, Lance heard the Lord speak to his heart and say to him, "Go outside and the first person you see, I want you to show him the video. I am going to heal him!"

Lance was, at first startled, but with his renewed faith, and vision, he was quickly obedient. At first, he was thinking the Lord would lead him to someone with a headache or another minor health problem. However, the first person Lance saw was a young man on a board with wheels, something like a wide skateboard, kneeling on it and pushing himself around with his hands. The young man was totally crippled from his knees down. He had been this way since he was six.

Lance was more than mildly surprised when he saw the young man on the skate platform. The man was begging and had come from a poor village. Lance said his lower legs hung like noodles when he picked him up. He was twenty-five years old, but about four foot eight inches in height, and he did look much younger.

Lance asked him if he would come to his apartment and look at a video of how God healed and he said, "Yes;" although, he said, he had never even heard of a God!

With some local friends, Lance carried the man upstairs to his fourth floor apartment. The group watched the video. All of them had their faith built. The tape was not just the preaching of a man, but through praise and worship, the tangible presence of the Lord was felt by all.

After watching the tape and seeing many people give testimonies of being healed in the meeting, the group was now ready to pray for the young man. Lance said later, that his faith came from hearing the Lord and simply doing what he said to do.

They began to pray with expectancy, and continued to pray for about fifteen minutes. The battle of faith really started here. Nevertheless, they kept on praying more intensely. Lance said they experienced some real doubt but kept on praying, kept on being obedient and persevering.

After about forty-five minutes, Lance could feel the presence of God coming to his arm, which he described as a warm, almost electric-like feeling. Oh, what joy filled his heart.

The healing presence of the Lord started touching the young man and went to his legs. There was great rejoicing going on. They asked the young man to stand up. Remember, this young man had atrophied muscles in his legs for nineteen years , and so this was a slow process.

He stood tentatively, and then straightened-up, and in a few minutes took his first steps. He could feel his legs getting stronger, and in a little while he was walking normally. Later, they took him out to a running track, and he ran around the track many times, barefooted.

He had not owned a pair of shoes for many years so the brothers and sisters went out and bought him some socks and shoes! There are many in the area, who will testify of this man's amazing healing. To say the least, this young man received Jesus as his Lord and Savior.

The Lord continued to use Lance that year in many healings, because of his faith in the Lord and his obedience. He and his wife now live on another continent, carrying on the work of the Lord. Lance has published a book about this amazing healing and it is blessing people with the faith, hope, and love of our heavenly Father. Glory to God for the great things He has done!

"The blind see and the lame walk" (Matthew 11:5).

Seventy-Eight:
FINDING TRUE LOVE: Anna's Test

When I was about five years old my grandmother died. My father took me to the cremation site to observe the actual cremation. Obsessing can be a common practice in the third-world country in which I lived.

Relatives watching the cremation really want to know that their loved ones have been professionally disposed of. As a young girl, I was badly shocked to actually see my grandmother's dead body being burned. I began worrying about my death because I was afraid of being burned like my grandmother. This greatly bothered me for several years and made me very upset.

At age seven years old, while I was walking home from school one day, I thought about my grandmother's cremation and how I could avoid dying.

Suddenly, I heard a quiet, almost inaudible voice say to me, "Don't be afraid, you will never die, you are different."

I looked up into the sky and felt very peaceful. I knew nothing about God at the time. I didn't know who had spoken to me, but I firmly believed I would never die. From that day on, I never thought about dying.

The next year, I started thinking about the value of my life. Why was I here? What purpose did my life serve? I just didn't know. This was too big a question for me to answer at that age. I had been taught to work hard so then I would have everything I needed, but deep-down in my heart, I knew that this was not the true goal of my life.

When I was a teenager, I started thinking about a man to marry some day, so he could show me the value of my life. From then on, I had many boyfriends, but they had no answers. I still felt empty.

I was a good student, but I knew the real value of life was not to just find a job and live to old age. Later on, I was married for three years and divorced. I was still seeking.

Next, I lived with a young man. I had a daughter by him. After a short time he left. It was very disappointing. So I continued longing to know the meaning and value of my life.

In 1987, I joined a Buddhist cult. The leader said they could take me to heaven. The only thing I received through my association with them was horrible, devilish dreams.

Now, I cried out to God in Heaven and an unnatural peace came over me. This was the very first time I called out to God. In 1992, I moved back home with my parents. I met a Christian who shared his faith with me. Later, I met an older Christian who shared that people are away from God because of their sin, but there is forgiveness, cleansing for our sinful heart through the death of Jesus Christ, God's own Son. I opened my heart and received Jesus' work for me.

At thirty-eight years of age, I found what I had always been looking for - the meaning and value of my life - I found it through Jesus. I knew without a doubt, that I would never die spiritually. I would live with Jesus forever!

> "He that believes on me, though he were dead, yet shall he live" (John 11:12).

Seventy-Nine:
DAD'S MOUNTAINTOP EXPERIENCE

It was a sunny day in March, 1986, and I was standing with my eight-year- old son on top of Table Rock Mountain in South Carolina. The view was truly endless that day, as if you could see a hundred miles in every direction, and it was beautiful to see.

"Rivers," I said to my son, as we looked at the hills and colors and clouds that seemed endless, "God made all of this, everything you see. And he did it with a word. He said it and it happened. And what we see is just a very small part of the world.

When you get older there are people who will tell you that God did not do it because God does not exist. Do not believe them. They are wrong. God made everything, including you and me."

You don't know what a young boy will remember, but I hoped it would make an impression that would last a lifetime. We looked a few more minutes, then turned to go back down the mountain it had taken us all morning to climb, over four thousand feet, some of it rocky, some of it muddy, some of it very steep.

Rivers and I were the last ones off the mountain that day. There was no one behind us, and no one in sight head of us.

About thirty minutes after we started down the mountain, the sky drew dark and cloudy. Suddenly there was a bolt of lightning in the sky around us and a tremendous clap of thunder. Rivers had been skipping down the trail several feet ahead of me when this happened. Instantly, he was at my side wanting my arm around him.

"You feel safe when Dad is holding you?" I asked him. He nodded vigorously.

"Well, the only reason either one of us is safe is because God has his arms around both of us. Remember that."

Another thought to plant in his young mind.

As we continued down the mountain, it began to rain, but we kept walking. It would be dark in a couple of hours and we had a long way to go, at least two hours. After a few minutes, the rain stopped.

However, we could not go any faster; in fact, we were going slower.

My right leg had begun to hurt and to go stiff. It was cramping badly, from my toes to my hip. I did not say anything to Rivers at first, but soon I had to explain why I could not walk more than a hundred feet without stopping to massage my leg.

Finally, I called him to come and feel my leg. It was like a board - ankle, calf, knee, thigh - it was hard all over, anywhere you touched it. I explained the problem to him and that we would be moving slowly. There was nothing I could do about my leg and it was increasingly painful to walk.

I realized that at the pace we were going, we would not make it down the mountain before it got dark. We had no flashlight and could not see the trail in the dark. We would be stranded on the side of the mountain with no way to tell anyone where we were.

My wife grew concerned, told the park ranger we had not come back, and they created a search party to come up the trail in the dark looking for us. And when they found us, they would have to carry me down the mountain. A lot of people were worried and put to trouble because of me and this stupid leg.

As I sat on a large rock, rubbing my leg and trying to make it bend, I knew I couldn't walk much further.

Without even thinking about it, I bowed my head and closed my eyes and I prayed with my whole heart: "Lord, I've never prayed a prayer like this for myself, or really for anyone else. I know, Lord, that you can fix my leg, and I'm asking you to do that, Lord. In the name of Jesus, please heal my leg so that I can make it to the bottom of this mountain with my son."

That was all I said. Instantly, I felt a ball of heat deep in my thigh, in the middle of my leg. In seconds, the heat began to flow up my thigh and down through my knee and the calf of my leg into my foot. It was an incredible feeling, physically, but I will never be able to describe the spiritual impact of feeling God's presence as he touched me and healed me.

In a matter of seconds, my leg was normal! I stood up and my put weight on it. I lifted it and moved it around. I took a few steps.

There was no pain. I could walk, I could even run.

I called my son to come and see my leg, to touch what had been brick hard, and see that it was normal again. He asked me what happened, why it was better.

I said, "Because I asked God to fix it so you and I could get down this mountain. I knew he could. I asked him to, and he did it. Don't ever forget what happened here today. There is no medicine that a doctor could give me that would have fixed my leg that fast. You have seen what God can do."

We made it the rest of the way down the mountain with no further problems, arriving back at our cabin before dark. If we hadn't told them, the family would never have known that there was a problem.

My leg was completely normal. Doctors have told me that it would take injections, massages, and probably two to three hours for medicine to have restored my leg. There was no medicine or technique that could have done it in seconds.

Was it a miracle? It was to me! God answered my prayer. He did for my body what doctors and medicine could not have done. Without him, I could not have walked another step that day. With him, I can walk through life knowing he is with me every step of the way.

> "He shall call upon me, and I will answer him: I will
> be with him in trouble; I will deliver him, and honor
> him" (Psalm 91:15).

Eighty:
DO YOU KNOW WHERE YOU WILL SPEND ETERNITY?

"Do you know where you will spend eternity?" What a question to ask somebody. Yet, this same question was asked by a man in Perth, Australia to thousands of people over the years in a famous tourist lane of this Western Australian city.

The Lord called this faithful Christian brother to stand in a doorway just off this lane, and when people approached, he would simply step out and ask them this most important question. I'm sure he received some startled looks, berating by some and just plain neglect and rejection by others. But this man did this for 30 years. Thirty years! He would share his faith in conventional ways in other areas, but in this one place he would ask this one question, "Do you know where you will spend eternity?"

Many years later at a convention, approximately six thousand full-time workers for the Lord would gather in one place for a series of meetings in the United States. One of the nights, the host of the meeting started to go around and ask the ministers how they came to the Lord, and asking them for a brief testimony of how they got into the ministry.

After several testimonies, one pastor stood up and said he was on his honeymoon in Perth, Australia, when a man came up to him and asked him and his bride, "Do you know where you will spend eternity?"

The man didn't answer him, but it bothered him so much, that it ruined his honeymoon. He went back to the States with this nagging question in his mind.

Finally, he got a Bible and started reading it, talked to some Christians and received Christ as his Savior. Shortly after that, he felt led to go to Bible School.

After graduating, he went on to enter the ministry. After the man in this meeting shared his testimony, about 40 hands went up across the auditorium. All of them shared that the same man spoke to them and asked them the same question!

Before the man in Australia died, someone told him of the many he had reached.

> " Cast your bread upon the waters, for you will find
> it after many days" (Ecclesiastes 11:1).

What God's Word Has to Say about Salvation

" Behold, I was brought forth in iniquity, and in sin my mother conceived me" (Psalm 51:5).

"I acknowledge my sin unto thee, and mine iniquity have I not hid. I said, I will confess my transgressions unto the LORD; and you forgave the iniquity of my sin. Selah" (Psalm 32:5).

"That if you confess with your mouth, "Jesus is Lord," and believe in your heart that God raised him from the dead, you will be saved. 10For it is with your heart that you believe and are justified, and it is with your mouth that you confess and are saved" (Romans 10:9, 10).

"Whosoever therefore shall confess me before men, him will I confess also before my Father which is in heaven. 33But whosoever shall deny me before men, him will I also deny before my Father which is in heaven" (Matthew 10:32, 33).

Therefore, if anyone is in Christ, he is a new creation; old things have passed away; behold, all things have become new. 18Now all things are of God, who has reconciled us to Himself through Jesus Christ, and has given us the ministry of reconciliation" " 2 Corinthians 5:17, 18).

As you have read these true stories of the living God's miraculous intervention in the lives of men and women, people who are just like you, perhaps you felt you would like to experience that kind of relationship with God Almighty. If you would like to know how you can have such a relationship, it starts by praying the following simple prayer, sincerely, out loud and from your heart. You can do that in the privacy of your own room, but in the presence of God and his angels. This is the first, but essential, step to a new, better life .

Dear Heavenly Father,

I have come to understand I have been living my life away from You and Your Word. I now acknowledge I am what your Word calls a "sinner" because I have missed your desire for my life as my loving Father. It is now my desire to stop living that lifestyle and to turn completely to You for your direction and help in how I should live my life for the rest of my days.

Therefore I confess that I believe your only Son Jesus Christ is Lord. I believe in my heart and now confess with my mouth that Jesus was crucified, buried, and raised from the dead, and now He lives at your right hand just as the Bible says. I invite Him into my heart, and I give Him Lordship of my life. I am sincerely sorry for my sins, and I now accept that You, Father, will forgive me of all my sins, right now, without any condemnation. From this point, I will practice the principles taught in Your Word, the Bible.

I believe that I am now born again, that the old things in my life have passed away, and I have by faith become a new creation in Christ Jesus. I am your child; I am a Christian. Thank you, Father.

In Jesus' name. Amen.

Congratulations!! You are now a full citizen of the Kingdom of God, with a new start in life. Your sins have been forgiven and forgotten (See Psalms 103:2-12).

We welcome you into the family of God. Please write to us and tell us of your decision . We would be delighted to send you other information about how to progress in your new Christian life; and, please, share your story with us. It may end up in another volume of 80 Adventures with God . For now , do these three things to get started...

Read the Bible every day. Begin with the Book of John. It's a good place to start. Begin praying, talking with your Heavenly Father daily, about everything. Speak to Him from your heart. Third, find a good Bible- teaching, Bible-believing Christian Church near you. There are other steps, but this is a good foundation for your new beginning.

About the Author
ED COLTON

Ed Colton has had a varied career in missionary work since 1976, having ministered in three continents. His main work has been to train and source many nationals in Asia and other countries to reach their own people.

While living in one of the Far Eastern countries for six years, he and his wife Sherry were a Worldreach Center. Another primary ministry they are involved in is providing funding for orphans who need surgeries, upgrading facilities, and assisting in adoptions. Now they travel to the Far East to carry on these vital works for the Lord. In the United States, Ed and Sherry do evangelistic work and train others to do the same.

Your purchase of this book will help them carry on their work for the Lord.

Mr Colton is a member of CHURCH of HIS PRESENCE DAPHNE, Alabama.

www.ingramcontent.com/pod-product-compliance
Lightning Source LLC
Chambersburg PA
CBHW071743120626
46550CB00002B/644